Ablaze in

Ablaze in Appalachia

A Social Approach to a Forgotten Culture

David R. Messer, MSW, CSSW

Book cover provided by Jill York and Printworks, Inc. Grayson, Kentucky

Author photo by Bonnie Barker. Olive Hill, Kentucky

Visit www.booksurge.com to order additional copies.

Ablaze in Appalachia

Table of Contents

AUTHOR BIOGRAPHY

❧

David R. Messer, MSW, CSSW

❧

David R. Messer is a Graduate of the University of Kentucky with a Master of Social Work Degree and is a Certified School Social Worker through the Kentucky Department of Education. He has earned a Bachelor of Science Degree in Theology and Youth Ministry from Baptist Bible College and is currently an Assistant Professor of Social Work and Field Practicum Coordinator at Kentucky Christian University. In the Collegiate realm, he has provided Adjunct teaching and practicum supervision at both the Bachelor and Masters level for the University of Kentucky, Morehead State University and Kentucky Christian University.

Mr. Messer has worked with children and families for 30 years in both urban cities such as Indianapolis and Detroit and in the Appalachian foothills of Kentucky through coaching athletics teams, church ministry and school social work. As a school social worker, he was the founder and Director of the Olive Hill Family Resource Center in Kentucky for 14 years where he has served as Regional Representative, Secretary, Editor and Vice-President for the State Coalition.

In regard to social advocacy, the author has served as chair for the Governor's Multi-disciplinary Task Force on Child Sexual Abuse, current Welfare Secretary for the Salvation Army, Former Chair of the Citizens Foster Care Review Board, and member of the Carter County Domestic Violence Task Force, Hispanic Coalition and Champions Against Drugs.

Mr. Messer is author and trainer of *Prevent*: a behavioral management approach to deescalating violent and aggressive behavior. He presents his professional development training to schools and agencies as a caring approach module for the prevention of crisis. His newest endeavor is to provide consultation to community and school management teams in the development of individual crisis plans.

PREFACE

❧

I always wondered if there was some mystical or miraculous phenomenon that caused a whole generation of people to want to return to the mountains of Appalachia. As a city boy, I grew anxious as summer came. I knew my trip to Grandpa and Grandma Yorke's house in Virginia would be full of excursions to the fields and streams of the Appalachian Mountains. Nothing tasted better on those summer mornings at Grandma's than her home made apple butter on a hot biscuit. I enjoyed dressing up in my uncle's old army shirts and sneaking off to the woods like the mountain men I knew they were. My cousins and I would always get a good "whoopin" for throwing the apples that came off of Grandma's trees. I remember my uncles coming home from the coalmines all black from head to finger tip. The cellar where they kept the furnace coal and antique tools of years gone by was a favorite place to play.

Nostalgia still soars in my mind, as I hold my Grandpa Messer's 1907 Winchester 22. This heirloom, given to me by my father, helps me remember Grandpa's love for the outdoors, the hills, and the thrill of a hunt. I am sure no grandchild in the world could have been any cleaner than I. Especially after surviving Grandma Messer's scrub-a-dub-dub in the big wash tub. And not even the finest roller coaster could match the thrill of riding in the car down Spring Hill where my Grandparent's lived.

Whether it was hunting squirrel in Virginia, catching trout on a rainy day in West Virginia, playing in coal dust, or reminiscing about my father's birth and roots in Kentucky, my family from the mountains saw to it that this city boy had a chance to experience the culture of Appalachia.

Now that I am grown and have a family of my own, I find myself back "home" in the foothills of the Appalachia Mountains of Kentucky. I have wonderful memories of teaching my daughters how to string a bow, fire a rifle that dates back to when their great-grandfather held it in his own hands, and how to follow a deer through the same hills as their family did in years gone by. Now that I have a grandson, I look forward to many years of sharing those same experiences with him. My children will long remember their Great-grandma Duncan's hard rock candy and being rocked to sleep on her front porch on Rattlesnake Ridge. They have experienced Appalachian culture at it's finest with it's Sorghum making, quilting, and home made butter. And let's not forget making cookies with Grandma, and learning to sew. Tall tales? Grandpa Greenhill had more tales than Carter had pills! It is only now that I understand what that mysterious pull is all about. I wouldn't want to raise my children anywhere else in America.

ABSTRACT

❧

Appalachia is Ablaze with colorful people and a rich heritage, but Appalachia has its dark side too. For twenty-two years I have counseled children and families in Appalachia, and have found that they are a people who are in desperate need of social change. As a Social Worker, I had to come to the realization that I could not affect change in an entire culture. Change had to occur one person at a time. I live daily with the frustration of cycles of poverty and lack of fit. Who are the Appalachian people? What are their roots? This book will help you understand those questions. At times it may be detailed. Don't skip those lines for between them lay the answers to: "Who are the Appalachian people, and what are their roots?" The Appalachian people are a blended culture, much like our entire country. "The melting pot of nations" is a phrase that not only refers to the United States of America, but also to Appalachia. I like to think of Appalachia as a salad bowl. In a salad, everything is blended together, but maintains its own flavor. That is Appalachia!

You may have picked up this book out of a curiosity for the Appalachian people. Your vision for social change may be Urban America or the suburbs that dot our countryside. Whatever your vision for social change, there must be an urgency to know the people with whom you work and the battlefields on which they fight. This book is a delving into the Culture of the Appalachian people. From the shores of California, to the Eastern coast, the Appalachian people have migrated. From the lakes in the Northern United States, to the southern most tips of our country, the Appalachian people have carried with them their values and beliefs. This book is a celebration of the Appalachian culture, which brought one social worker back home. It will take a look at the goodness of fit in a people...
   ...whose traditional value system is an expression of their culture
   ...whose stereotyping has not held them back
   ...whose heritage is multi-cultural and reflects the true crayon box of a nation
   ...whose religion fashions their way of life
   ...whose extreme beliefs create social dilemma
   ...whose self-determination and independence is a cornerstone of the family
   ...whose humor and light heartedness has become a healing balm for hard times
   ...whose culture passes on a lifestyle of altruism, hospitality and humility.

In a book that will follow in the future, I will focus on social work practice and specific interventions for issues pertinent to the Appalachian people. But for the present time, this book is about knowing a people well enough to effect social change in a forgotten culture. Social Workers, who seek to empower any culture, must have an intimate knowledge of its people. We must get a vision. A man of great wisdom once said: "Where there is no vision the people parish." (Bible, Proverbs 19:18)

Any great General will tell you that the difference between winning and losing a battle is knowing your opposition. Although I am not a General, I have learned some valuable lessons about the oppositions to social change and empowerment in Appalachia. The battle scars upon children and social workers alike come from wars won and lost. Those scars are not always visible scars. The fight for social change in Appalachia is not always an easy fight. Most professionals will tell you to detach yourself from your work. Don't take your work home with you. If you are a true social worker, the empty stomachs, dirt floors, no electric or water, incest, and abuse seem to always become our own battles. Appalachia is a forgotten mission field. Appalachia is a forgotten culture.

This book will address the lack of fit and social conflicts of a culture still locked in time. This is a social worker's look at his people. As you read, you will recognize social theory without the jargon. If we are going to affect social change as professionals, we need wisdom about the people we desire to empower. Another wise man once said, "If any man lack wisdom, let him ask of God who giveth to all men liberally." (Bible, James 1:5) Let us take that approach to social work and empowering the people of Appalachia. **We must know them to empower them. If we want to empower them, we must love them. If we love them, we must reach out to them! GOD, GIVE US WISDOM!**

This book is dedicated to my little shadow, "mini-me" my first grandchild:
Nathaniel Douglas Johnson

"May you grow strong and free in the hills of Appalachia! May you hold to a strong belief and value system that is pleasing to God! May music, art and laughter fill your life with joy! May you always invest your life in the lives of others! May you develop into a strong, independent man, proud of who you are and who God has made you to be!
May you live life with a humble spirit, a willing heart to serve and a caring soul!

I love you!
Pawpaw

CHAPTER ONE

A HALLMARK OF APPALACHIAN CULTURE:
The traditional value system as an expression of culture

WHAT DO YOU VALUE? When you use the words "traditional value system" you often think about the battles that rage between religion and politics. In recent years, a catch phrase for many campaigns has been the belief in a traditional value system. But, what is a traditional value system? This author's crutch for understanding comes from Mr. Webster. His book states that tradition is the handing down of information, beliefs, and customs by word of mouth or by example from one generation to another without written instruction. It is an inherited pattern of thought or action, and cultural continuity in social attitudes and institutions. He further enlightens us by explaining that a value is something held as intrinsically valuable or desirable (Webster, 1977) Social workers are well aware of the general systems theory that allows us to take a holistic approach to working with people. This book is that look at Appalachian Culture.

"A traditional value system is when an individual or group of individuals accepts and practices a particular belief or tradition."

In Appalachian terms, a traditional value system is...."I believe what I believe because Great-grandpa said our family has always believed this way. I do what I do because this is the way our family has done it for years. If it was good enough for them, it's good enough for me. There's nothing you can say to change my mind. If I am wrong, at least I'll die a happy man."

The value system of the Appalachian people is a product of many things. Among the first is a history of outlooks on life and beliefs that have been past down from generation to generation. Why is it that my children eat ketchup on scrabbled eggs, or dip their Oreos in milk instead of twisting them apart? Why do children often follow in their parent's footsteps with careers or family businesses? The answer is tradition.

"Appalachia is Ablaze with tradition, and not all tradition is bad! Tradition is the landmark of our culture. Because of that strong grasp on tradition, the people of Appalachia are strongly rooted."

They are rooted to the point of willing to stand "toe to toe" with anyone who may come between them and their right to believe "their own way". "Their own way" refers to the desire to live the simple life. Later in this book, I will describe their outlooks on life and their "beliefs". But for now, we can say the Appalachian value system is strong and proud (Jones, 1994).

The Appalachian people have been described using many terms. Among them are southern highlanders, mountain people, survivors, strugglers, culturally challenged, backwoods folk, snake-oil peddlers, hillbillies, hicks, and rednecks. Many of the names they have been tagged with reflect their tradition of challenging the advancements of society. Some names reflect society's stereotype of a culture that has not had the advantages to put a foot forward. Some names reflect their cultural history (Billings, 2000).

However you chose to describe the Appalachian people, the traditional rural family places a high value on the things of the past. After 30 years of ministry and 14 years of school social work, I would be a rich man if I had a dime for every time I've heard "We've never done it that way before", or "We've done it this way for years". That, my friend, is the true expression of tradition. If something is new, it is often met with skepticism. However, they are not so proud as to deny what is good for the family. That strong tie to tradition has been their stronghold of survival.

"Tradition is safe and comfortable. When there are tried and true traditions that produce a goodness of fit, any culture will hold strong to them!"

The area of Appalachia in which I live is very strongly Democratic. Our voters may not be able to tell you that they have either liberal or conservative views on political issues. They per chance may have not voted since JFK. However, if you ask them why they are a registered Democrat, they will tell you: "Our family has always been registered that way". One Autistic child I have worked with for years approached me in a local restaurant and declared: "Guess what Mr. David Messer? I'm 18. I'm a Democrat. I voted this year!" Bless his heart. He may not fully comprehend our political system, but he knew the tradition of his family! This tie with tradition is not exclusive to our Appalachian culture, but it is strong within the history of the area. Placing value on the past is a jewel long missed in the family unit today. The sense of family that will be spoken of later is also a strong part of Appalachia.

I am often faced with clients who would rather just be left alone. They cherish their privacy and solitude. For generations they have had to fend for themselves, relying only on self and family. As a result, they have become strong, self-reliant and self-determined. These are the traditional values past down from generation to generation. Social work values and ethics today hold strong to these same premises of self-determination for the client.

"This rural tradition of self-determination and self-reliance is written into the very Code of Ethics established by the National Association of Social Workers." (NASW, 1999).

Our profession must look close at this strong spirit of self-determination as a valuable tool in case management of clients with strong ties to their Appalachian culture. To affect social change among the Appalachian people, we must understand their traditional value system. We must know the systems at work in their lives. We must take a holistic approach if we are going to work with a culture ablaze with tradition. Social workers must accentuate the strengths of a culture strong with traditional values and pride.

So what is Appalachia and what is it's beginning? While researching the history of any town, river or territory you will find that they often carry different names than what they carry today. Appalachia is one of those territories. From the time the first settlers came to this area, people have questioned where the Appalachian territory begins and where it ends. What we now call the Southern Appalachian region was better known as the Unakas in the early years of our country. If you do a quick study on the word Unaka, you are not likely going to find it. What you will find is the more recent names for this mountain range. Those names are the Allegheny or Alleghenies. One of my favorite childhood characters was Daniel Boone. I remember watching Hank Parker in his series on television, and hearing him say: "I'm the toughest man west of the Alleghenies". This is the first history of the area. The words Apalche and Apalchen have been found on many early Spanish maps. When the Spanish wrote about our region, it usually referred to an area between Florida and Virginia. When looking at many of the existing maps of the new world and its colonies stretching south, these mountains were the one geographical constant within most of the states in the new Republic.

In one way or another, the terms Appalachians or Alleghenies were interchanged depending upon where you lived. To add to the individualism for its inhabitants, parts of the Appalachians were given even different names. The name Blue Ridge Mountains is often used in Virginia to refer to the middle ridges of the Appalachians. Another term, Great Smoky Mountains, refers to the mountains along the border of Tennessee and North Carolina. (Drake, 2001). Other names have come up during the years to define the area. As people of other nationalities moved into the mountains, they adopted names such as the Southern Mountains or the Southern Highlands. Various divisions have taken place over the years where the mountains were used as boundaries for their conflicts. These mountains were used to divide larger regions of a young United States. Geographically, the mountains divided Virginia from Kentucky and North Carolina from Tennessee. Economically, the mountains divided the settlers. Those who settled on the east side of the mountains focused their trade and well being upon the East toward the Atlantic Ocean. Those West of the mountain range focused their trading opportunities on the west side toward the Mississippi River (Eller, 1982).

Not only did the mountains divide a region geographically and economically, but it also divided them over social issues. Because the mountains were outpost areas of the region, there was less need for slaves to work the small farms. Many of the settlers were themselves indentured slaves. The last thing they wanted to be a part of was slavery. Slavery was never accepted in the hilly regions of Western Virginia. When Virginia seceded from the Union in 1861, they seceded themselves from their own state and formed West Virginia. The state of Tennessee suffered the same social differences. Eastern Tennessee and Western Tennessee were divided over slavery as well. They held strong as a state, yet they still stand divided today over many other political differences. This crisis also carried into the strongholds of Western North Carolina causing a sectional crisis for its people. Never has one topic, such as slavery, divided so many regions (Inscoe, 1989). How then will we define Appalachia?

"Some people may define it with a simple statement: Appalachia is a culture of mountain people living in rural areas void of society and different from anyone else in the nation."

If you accept that definition, then you have the wrong picture of Appalachia. Appalachia is not just the mountain and rural areas. Does Appalachia include the large cities of the region? There are large cities along the low-lying rivers of Appalachia like Charleston, West Virginia, Harrisburg, Pennsylvania, Knoxville and Chattanooga, Tennessee. If we do include those large cities with populations of over 100,000, we must also include larger cities such as Lexington, Kentucky, and even larger Southern cities. These cities are even higher in altitude than many of those secluded mountain hollows. It is clear that Appalachia is hard to define. The bottom line is this:

"Appalachia can not be defined as a matter of land, ethnicity, education, or even dialect. One major marker for our culture is the traditional value system of the Appalachian people. Years of study still may not allow us to put a finger on a definition, but we can learn to understand the root of Appalachia: it's people."

CHAPTER TWO

THOSE POOR ILLITERATE HILLBILLIES:
Living above the stereotypes of society

Hillbilly". I am not sure who originated the word, but it is a name society has been quick to hang on families living at a lower socioeconomic level in the mountains. Many typecast these secluded families to be more like billy goats than people, thus the name.

"A more affluent society often falls to the misconception that mountain people are unlearned, ignorant and illiterate people. Why do you think mountain cultures are an easy target for discrimination by a 'cultured' society?"

When society doesn't understand something, it tends to criticize. Criticism soon turns into discrimination. Discrimination? Yes, and quite acceptable in our society. What is it society doesn't understand? It is why anyone would choose to live a secluded life? Their choice of an isolated lifestyle sometimes breeds misunderstanding. It's not normal. But I ask: "who gets to define normal?" Because someone does not live up to lifestyle "norms" of a mainstream society, it makes it acceptable to target them for discrimination and prejudice. When is it acceptable to make fun of a culture? Never. Just like other ethnic cultures, the "hillbilly" is often the blunt of insensitive jokes. Call it my own bias, but the Appalachian people are one of the only ethnic groups that are "open game" for heartless remarks and sell out comedy acts. An ethnic group? Yes, and one rich with pride and character.

"Although society often looks at ethnicity as one race or nationality, I view our blended Appalachian people as an ethnic group of their own with no regard to race or ethnicity".

Tell a joke in public about minorities, or even religion and it is in poor taste. Tell a joke about two rooms and a path, or a barefoot, pregnant hillbilly, and it seems to be funny. Most of the families I work with in Appalachia fall into that category. One of my parents specifically comes to mind. She is a 30-year-old single mother of seven. She works hard to break out of the "mold" our rural town has placed her in. She is often the blunt of "the baby factory" jokes by many. What their whispering does not say is that she had worked hard for

8 years to keep an abusive marriage alive. She found the strength to stand up in court and say "I won't take it anymore". She took a stand and moved out on her own. Now she has found help under Welfare reform, and works hard to better herself in a new job. I often stop for breakfast at that little restaurant to check on her. She's made the best out of the worse. Should someone make a joke of her self-determined success? You decide for yourself.

During the 1800s there arose many authors and journalist who found Appalachia as a source for their colorful comedy and humorous writings. They pictured the Appalachian people as a culture living in degrading life-styles and void of moral values. They were painted as hopeless, helpless, and too proud to ask for help. Their lot in life, according to the writings about them, was ignorance and lack of education. The region was initially described in terms of romantic wonder. By the mid 1890s the stereotype had expanded to American literature. Newspaper comic strips such as Lit'l Abner and Snuffy Smith promoted an image of the poor ignorant hillbilly. The television, with shows such as The Beverly Hillbillies and Ma and Pa Kettle, perpetuated the stereotype. Probably most notable among the stories of Appalachia is the Hatfield and McCoy feud. It's more than just a "hillbilly" story. The Industrial Revolution in America brought with it the great need for coal. It became the fuel that made Appalachia an economic power. Because it is the greatest source of coal in America, the Appalachian Mountains resounded with the cry for coal. Stripping the Appalachian Mountains of its coal and natural resources changed the social and economic face of our people for all time. Here is one of the saddest facts of all. Our Appalachian ancestors didn't realize the wealth that was really theirs. Imagine owning one of the richest mines in America. You then sell it to someone for several hundreds of dollars. You are then asked to turn around and work in the same mine, which produces billions of dollars in coal. For many of our Appalachian people, this is exactly what happened. Many rural families sold their land and mineral rights to mining companies for mere pennies per acre. Being use to hard work, the mountain people soon became laborers, rather than CEO's and owners of those large mining companies built on the lands they once owned.

Many of our southern highland families struggled over the rich natural resources in the mountains and hillsides of Appalachia. In American history and folklore, the story of the Hatfields and McCoys is one of those struggles which has come to symbolize the world's attitude about Appalachian culture. They view us as backwoodsmen who take things into their own hands. Yet, when you take a closer look at this infamous conflict between families, it tells a greater story than one might think. It is not just a story about two families' struggles. It goes deeper. It is about competition over property and personal rights. It was a feud whose outcome was about economic stability for the family. It was a feud that revealed to the world the self-determined, independent and proud spirit of a culture more bent on will than what was right (Eller 1982). The conflict begins with the loss of property. It extends to a perpetuating problem of our culture, and that is the "haves" and "have-nots". Coal companies were making large purchases of local timber and land for economic development in the Appalachian area. The feud was not only a preview of the bloody coalmine wars that would fill the 1900's, but also an example of families protecting their traditional mountain culture and family. Let me tell you the story and allow you to apply it to any other struggle between culture and society, whether urban or suburban of that era. This story will give you a reflection of conflict in rural America.

The Hatfield and McCoy conflict: a picture to the world

What was the real story? The first hint of trouble between the Hatfields and McCoys occurred in the fall of 1878 on the Kentucky side of the Tug Fork. Economic development had not yet made it here in our area of the Kentucky/West Virginia border. This area of Appalachia had been virtually untouched by industry. There were no coalmines, cities or towns. There were no riverboats and railroads. However, there were the Hatfields and McCoys. The feud between families began when Randolph McCoy accused Floyd Hatfield of stealing his hog. Theft of any kind of farm animal was a pretty grave offense in the wilderness. When Randolph McCoy decided to make a legal report to the local officials, you knew that trouble and discord had begun between these two families. Some Appalachian historians believe the more intense conflict started over the market for the rich timber in the region. The high quality hardwoods in the Southern Appalachians were in great demand in the early industrialization of America. Before the large timber corporations moved into the Tug Valley, the locals cut and marketed their own timber. William Anderson Hatfield, often called "Devil Anse", had been more successful than any other in the Tug Valley. Randolph McCoy and his family on the other hand had not been so lucky. Their attempt at the timber market was a struggle. Because of that, the McCoys felt the need to fight for every square piece of land and goods that they felt were theirs. Whatever problems arose between the two, Randolph McCoy attempted to resolve them through the legal system. The court ruled against Randolph McCoy in his complaint about the stolen hog. Thus the hard feelings between the clans intensified (Jones, 1974).

Almost identical to the Romeo and Juliet story, Devil Anse's son, Johnse, found love with a "fair maiden" on the other side of the river. Her name was Roseanna McCoy. When she became pregnant, and Johnse refused to marry her, you can imagine how the feud exploded. Three of Roseanne's brothers took matters into their own hands. They attacked and killed Ellison Hatfield in 1882. Because the Tug Fork (a branch of the Big Sandy River) is the boundary between Kentucky and West Virginia, the authorities on both sides refused to take responsibility for doing anything about the murder. The legal system failed to intervene. Devil Anse was not going to stand idle without something being done about the death of his brother, so he executed the three sons of Randolph McCoy.

Things were quiet for some time until a Pikeville lawyer named Perry Cline renewed the Hatfield-McCoy controversy. This young man had grown up in the Tug Valley and was a distant cousin of Randolph McCoy. As a young man, he got into a legal dispute with Devil Anse over five thousand acres of land. In short, Cline had lost the five thousand acres. (Spivak, 1980). In 1887, Cline invested his time and efforts to influence the legal system to re-open the five-year-old murder indictments against the Hatfields. He wanted the extradition process started again to bring the Hatfields to trial in Kentucky. As the family history goes, he thought the legal system wasn't working quickly enough. He hired a man who was called "Bad" Frank Philips to cross the Tug Fork into West Virginia and capture nine of the Hatfields. That was not a wise move, for it began several small skirmishes and murder attempts on both sides of the feud. At the end of the skirmishes, there were two of Randolph McCoy's children dead and their home on Blackberry Fork, Kentucky burned to the ground. It was time for real action. The real issue now was a conflict between Kentucky and West Virginia. Governor E. Willis Wilson of West Virginia now issued a complaint against Kentucky for not extraditing the accused to West Virginia for trial. The Governor appealed the matter to the Supreme Court of the United States, and in May of 1889, the Supreme Court decided against West Virginia. The nine Hatfields were tried in Pikeville, Kentucky. The feud was over by 1892. It had lasted 12 years and cost 12 lives. At the root of it all was a quest for economic stability for the family.

> *"The battles over land and natural resources in Appalachia were inevitable during a time when the doors for economic development opened in Kentucky and West Virginia. The modernization of our area was inevitable."*

If it were not the Hatfields and McCoys, it would have been the Smiths and Jones'. The story of the Hatfields and McCoys is an Appalachian story, but speaks of the constant socioeconomic struggles of the region. A timeline of the Hatfield and McCoy Conflict is available in Appendix A for further study.

Living above the stereotypes of society means getting a nation to understand that there is a culture of people who have selected isolation by choice. However you view the Appalachian people, life in the wilderness and isolation by choice has made us different from most other Americans. We value things differently than most of the world. That Appalachian value system influences attitude and behavior. It **is** different from the norm, and similar to the value system of an earlier America. "Hillbilly" may be the name we carry, but the people of the hills and hollows simply take a different look at life than a modern society. What is seen as a "modern" value system to society is seen as intrusive to mountain people. What may be traditional for mountain people is seen as backward, isolated, and "strange" in some way. Isn't that what diversity is all about?

> *"Social work in Appalachia is about accepting my diverse beliefs about life. Even if I choose a backward lifestyle, it's the role of the change agent to meet me where I am and take me where I need to be within my own value system."*

Living above the stereotypes of society means calling a nation to acceptance of diversity that is not racial, but cultural. Some of our strongest values are based on a personal religious belief, strong family unity, being our own individual, strong self-determination, pride, contentment with our "state of affairs", love for the beauty in nature, sense of humor, being a good neighbor, and love of country. In what we call a modern society, the Appalachian people have learned how to be more diverse than ever. Whether those who grew up in Appalachia now live in a rural or urban setting, we all still share the same values. You can take the man out of the mountain, but you can't take the mountain out of the man. We have created a proud heritage. You can't separate our present from our past.

Living above the stereotypes means challenging society to understand the struggles that define our culture. Appalachia's great struggles began with its strongest resources of coal, oil, timber, and natural resources, which have vanished over the years. The strong rich resources of the Appalachian people are no longer strong nor are the people rich. After years of prosperity, most of the industries are gone. The landscapes are stripped yet beautiful, exploited yet underdeveloped. Our local brickyards once prosperous are now laid to ruin. Our textile factories are gone. Our coalmines are now empty and our strip mines dwindle (Billings 2001). Although the Appalachian region may be low socioeconomically, what we do have in Appalachia is a strong value for family, self-reliance and pride. These qualities are what have enabled us to rebound from hard times. Not bad for those labeled as the Snuffy Smiths of society.

The education system in the early foothills of Appalachia

The people of Appalachia are neither illiterate nor just a colorful colloquialism. Most of the families who migrated into the mountains were very literate. That was evident by the many letters, documents, and books that they possessed and wrote. Many of the Appalachian poets, such as Jesse Stewart (a one-room schoolhouse teacher and principal from my county in Kentucky) were quite educated and literate. Illiterate Hillbillies they were not. For generations people left formal education and valued this as one of their freedoms of choice. Much like the home-school movement of today, parents "schooled" their children at home. Often a small community would bring in a teacher to educate the children in their hollow or valley. Because of the small farming communities that were settled in our secluded foothills, there was a need for local "one-room" schools. With each school came diversity of grades and learning levels. The rise of these quaint one room schoolhouses became common (Rogers 1980). To bring it home a little closer, my own father-in-law was one of the last teachers at Rattlesnake School, which was one of the last one-room schools in Carter County, Kentucky. The students in the school were from farms that dotted the ridge road, one of which he married years later. Children once educated in those rural Appalachian schools had to often choose to stay at home to work the farm as times became hard. Once they did reach working age, the career options available were quite limited. That is still the case in most of our small communities. Because of these factors, there were and still are significant levels of poverty that affect the community, family, and our quality education (Rogers, 1980).

> *"The one-room schools and small community education efforts in Appalachia were faced with issues of significant poverty, limited resources and isolation in the hills. They struggled to prepare their students for the challenges of a modern society and worldly economy to which they were unfamiliar."*

As we continue to look at this bleak picture, the facts can not be mentioned enough. Young adults are relegated to working service jobs that dominate small towns. If you study the problems with work and unemployment, you find the best and the brightest moving away to find higher levels of education and the advancements of technology to etch out a career. This brain drain of our finest students is saddening. As with urban America, a large number of the jobs children were trained for were either in the area of farming or service. Our rural towns are plagued with jobs that pay low wages. The rise of single-parent families, few social services, and low levels of education in parents are only a few of the challenges faced by many rural Appalachian communities. Teachers and Principals in the turn of the century rural schools were generally younger, had fewer if any advanced degrees, were paid next to nothing and often did not major in the area they taught. One of the struggles of the rural school was keeping a teacher for any length of time. Held back by the high cost of education, less experienced educators, poverty, and limited job opportunities, the rural Appalachian schools faced huge challenges to prepare their students for the work force.

A social dilemma that faced the Appalachian area (and still does) is the rate at which children drop out of school. There are many reasons why students didn't prepare for college.

Many children were influenced to drop out of school. They were oriented to believe that their lot in life was to take care of the family or family farm. Few rural school dropouts ever returned to finish high school, and in turn were forced to lower their career aspirations and their dreams for the future. For those who did finish it was a victory. The possibilities of children in rural Appalachia ever entering college were often perceived as unrealistic. Perhaps it was because the local job availability did not require a college education, and in most cases the major roadblock for college education was the lack of money to attend. More specifically, there were few if any colleges accessible to children in rural counties. So, what is the outcome? College becomes a low priority and a luxury. It becomes an impossible mission. All, however, is not bleak. Even with the great social dilemmas that were present in the mountain community schools, there were many positive aspects about rural education in Appalachia. Let's look at a few of them.

> *"What these small rural communities may have lacked in helping resources, they often made up for with the supportive atmosphere of the whole community"*

The school is the place where community comes together. Just try to close a small school in most rural communities and you will have a mutiny on your hands. This mezzo system became the center of social exchange. There was a great push for families to be involved in school activities, which brought a sense of ownership to the community (Rogers, 1980). As family after family had to scratch out a living in the rural highlands by the sweat of their brow, education took a back seat. Doing what it took to survive became a number one priority. As our country spiraled headlong into the depression of 1941, families needed every available strong hand to work the fields, mines or factories. Illiterate hillbillies they are not. Uneducated out of necessity, they often were.

So who are we? What was it that brought us to the mountains? Where did we come from? When did our ancestors make that hard journey to the mountains of Appalachia? Why did they come? How did they spark a blazed trail through the mountains? Read on to discover this crayon box of culture we now call APPALACHIA? The bottom line is this:

> *"Living above the Stereotypes of Society is a social challenge. A person cannot be measured by where they live, but by who they are and who they become."*

CHAPTER THREE

THE ROOTS OF APPALACHIA:

The multi-cultural heritage that reflects the crayon box of a nation

Appalachia is ablaze with the multi-cultural influences of many nationalities. The United States prides itself in being the "Melting Pot" of nations. Appalachia is like a box of crayons mixed with individuals from every race, color, and creed. They have found a home in the mountains and foothills since our nation was discovered. This chapter takes a deep look at several of those cultures, the social issues of a developing nation, and how they shaped the Appalachian culture. Our first focus is the original Americans or first nations who possessed the lands and hills of Appalachia before we even arrived—the Native American Indian. Influences from their nations have made our country unique in every way.

"From our style of government, to our artistic expression, our country is ablaze with a multi-cultural heritage."

The True Americans: A history of the Appalachian Cherokee

Historians tell us that one of the first people of Appalachia were the Cherokee. Many influential Native American tribes exist in Appalachia, but I have chosen to focus on the Cherokee. The proud heritage passed on from generation to generation of American Indian is a spirit of survival and fortitude. Native Americans have made many contributions to our way of life in this country. As colonists entered the mountains of Appalachia, they depended greatly upon the help of the Cherokee for food and survival during difficult years on the frontier. Their expertise in agriculture helped colonists survive and prosper (Hatt, 1999). What did we offer in exchange? We offered one of the first social injustices in "American" history.

"With our invasion, we forced social change upon an already strong socialized nation. With change came attempts to expel, acculturate and annihilate an entire culture."

It was this social injustice perpetrated on Native Americans that forced them Westward or forced them into inevitable war and conflict. In the name of expansion, they were slowly forced to release their most important and valuable asset to our country: Land (Awiakta, 1978). History reveals a very bitter and tragic three-year war between the whites and the Cherokee here in Appalachia during the years 1759-1761. The Cherokee were a powerful people whose lands were mainly in Western Carolina, Northern Georgia and Alabama. The war against our First Nations raged throughout the wilderness as settlers made their way north along the borders of Virginia and the Carolinas. In June of 1761, the Cherokee made a good faith appeal to our nations system of justice and chose by their own hand to seek a peaceful resolution through a lawsuit filed with our nation's courts. Their hope was to bring about peace. During these few years of peace for the Cherokee, many settlers married people of the Cherokee nation. My great-great-grandfather was one whose wife was from that great nation, but she too was lost during this time of turmoil. The only knowledge we have of her is stories. We have no historical facts. It was 1838 when our government finally forced over 15,000 Cherokee westward to reservations. This tragic event, now called the Trail of Tears, left Appalachia with only the influences of a great nation (Burnett, 1890).

"A misuse of authority and a travesty in public policy took away the human rights of our First Nations people who possessed the land we now call our Appalachian home. Does public policy work for Native Americans? Please do a historical study on your own and then you decide if we used public policy and racial discrimination to advance a growing nations power, prestige and wealth. The origin, history and blend of the Southern Cherokee Nation are now just a silent part of our American history."

The last part of the 1700's and early 1800's was an era that saw a swell of people from all nations coming to America. Appalachia not only grew from the mixed marriages between the Cherokee and English, but also between the Cherokee and German, French, Irish, Scot-Irish and other settlers who came to the Appalachian region. Believe it or not those alliances were often encouraged among both the Cherokee and the United States Government. Because of the mix between American Indian and other immigrants to the Americas, there rose up a diverse leadership among the Cherokee Nation. Some were pure Cherokee, and some were of mixed blood. The most famous of these leaders were John Ross, Major Ridge, and his son John Ridge. John Ross was popular with the full-blooded Cherokee. On the other side, Major Ridge and his son John made it their life goal to stand up for the rights of the mixed blood Cherokee. They were not so entrenched in the "old ways" but were more progressive in their efforts to right the wrongs of their nation.

The tragic story of the Cherokee goes even deeper. During the late 1800's, the state of Georgia was one of the last of the original 13 Colonies to be organized. It was experiencing a great pressure to become a wealthy state. Many in leadership attributed that lack of wealth to the presence of the Cherokee. Other colonies had already begun to expand and annex larger masses of land. However, Georgia could only expand its boundaries as far as Atlanta. They were land locked because the bulk of fertile land was in the ownership of the Cherokee Nation. Naturally then, the grass began to look a little greener on the other side and the "gold nugget" of lands owned by the Indian nations became a possible solution to expanding their own wealth, power and territories (Mails, 1996).

"In an attempt to become wealthy, the physical and social annihilation of a strong culture seemed justifiable. Any culture that sets a priority to obtain wealth and power at the expense of civil rights is destined to failure, turmoil, injustice and a national legacy of racism and prejudice."

The resources of the Cherokee nation had been a long kept secret. When the colonists discovered their wealth, they made appeals to the U.S. Government to do away with the Cherokee's rights to own land within Georgia's territorial limits. Sadly, the U.S. Government agreed to do this in the year 1802. The U.S. Government didn't move quickly enough for the territorial leaders, and so history tells us Georgia passed their own laws to deny the rights of the Cherokee. Under new Georgia law, no Cherokee could own land or property. The State Government not only denied them the right to vote, but also prevented them from testifying in court in their own defense against a white man. The end result of Georgia's actions sealed the doom of the Cherokee who lived there. This violation of civil rights was not an uncommon practice in early American history, especially for these "First American's". With new state laws passed, the "non-native" residents of the territory of Georgia were given freedom to rob, beat, kill and slaughter Cherokee families without fear of repercussion from our U.S. Government or the State of Georgia. History often reveals to us the cruelty of our actions. In this case, it reveals that the state of Georgia allowed a bounty to be placed and provided protection under the law to those who killed a Cherokee. The state government's method of dividing the Indian land was through a sanctioned lottery system. This gave people the right to divide the lands owned by the Cherokee Nation. What makes this an atrocity is how they obtained the land. It was ownership by death. Cherokee tracts of land were given to any settler who would expel, or even kill, the Cherokee family living there. The settlers were then granted protection from the Georgia Militia and Georgia court system for their actions (Perdue, 1995).

When the Federal Government became involved, under orders from President Jackson and in defiance of the U.S. Supreme Court, the U.S. Army began to strongly enforce a Removal Act and population transfer which ordered more than 3,000 Cherokees to be rounded up. In the summer of 1838, the army loaded thousands of Cherokee into boats and sent them up the Tennessee, Ohio, Mississippi and Arkansas Rivers into Indian Territory. Many were held in prison camps awaiting their fate. In the winter of 1838-39, our history books record over 14,000 Cherokee were marched almost 1,000 miles through Tennessee, Kentucky, Illinois, Missouri and Arkansas into rugged territory. Many historians believe the numbers recorded were much understated. These are only estimates, for no one can truly count the true number who died on this tragic death march. For those who escaped along the way, their prize was refuge in the seclusion of the Appalachian Mountains and foothills. An estimated 4,000 Native Americans died along the trail. Many died from hunger. More died from exposure. The blankets from small pox casualties were given to the Cherokee and thus gross numbers died from a disease they had never been exposed to until "civilization" came their way. This journey became an eternal memory for the Cherokee. Today it is remembered as the Trail of Tears. The Cherokee came to call the event Nunahi-Duna-Dlo-Hilu-I or Trail Where They Cried (Mulligan, 1970).

A survivor story of the Trail of Tears

"Long time we travel on way to new land. People feel bad when they leave old nation. Women cry and make sad wails. Children cry and many men cry, and all look sad like when friends die, but they

say nothing and just put heads down and keep on go towards West. Many days pass and people die very much. We bury close by Trail." (National Historic Trail, 2007).

<u>An escort soldier's shares of the Cherokee journey north</u>

"We were eight days in making the journey (80 miles), and it was pitiful to behold the women & children who suffered exceedingly as they were all obliged to walk, with the exception of the sick.... I had three regular ministers of the gospel in my party, and...we have preaching or prayer meeting every night while on the march, and you may well imagine that under the peculiar circumstances of the case, among those sublime mountains and in the deep forest with the thunder often roaring in the distance, that nothing could be more solemn and impressive. And I always looked on with...awe, lest their prayers which I felt...ascending to Heaven and calling for justice to Him who alone can & will grant it...[might] fall upon my guilty head as one of the instruments of oppression."—Lt. L.B. Webster (Digital History, 2007).

<u>Trick or treaty?</u>

From the first day our government began to deal with the Cherokee nation, treaty after treaty was signed. Many of those treaties made promises that were never kept. This is not a book of the complete history of the Cherokee Nation. However, it is imperative that we look at how a nation like the United States so strong on civil rights did not always honor what is now so cherishes.

"In social work, we have strong beliefs about the necessity of public policy. We believe social change can be done through passing laws and protecting rights. This is why the treaties passed and never kept with the Cherokee Nation show that even public policy may not always effect change!"

The proud heritage passed on from generation to generation of First Nations people is a spirit of survival and fortitude. It was this fortitude that made the Cherokee press on toward what they thought would be a good life in Indian Territory on the Trail of Tears. Today, it is that same pride and spirit that directs a great nation on a new trail. That is the trail of hope and opportunity. Since their first contact with Anglo-Saxon settlers and other cultures of the world dating back to the 1500's, the Cherokee Nation stands historically as one of the most advanced tribes among Native Americans. As mentioned before, the Cherokee culture thrived for hundreds of years in the Appalachian Southeast before any contact was made with white men. Even with contact from the "civilized" world, the Cherokee society and culture developed quicker and stronger. With the influences of the "melting pot of nations", they soon grew into a strong bicultural nation and government (Mankiller, 1993).

Many of the great contributions made by Native Americans have been taken for granted. Appalachia's current financial stability rests upon the cash crops of corn and tobacco introduced to us by their culture. About 1.9 million people of Native American descent now live in the United States. The United States Government officially recognizes over 544 American Native tribes or groups. The biggest tribe, according to the Census Bureau figures, is the Cherokee nation numbering over 308,000. Within Appalachia there are over 80,000 Native Americans. Their influence upon our lives and culture is real and positive. Today, there is a greater appreciation for the Native American culture. Our Appalachian heritage owes a debt of gratitude to the influences of art, literature, theater and film by today's true Americans. A historical timeline of the Cherokee is available in Appendix B.

The English in America: Anglo-Americans in Appalachian history

The influence of Anglo-Americans has had more impact on American society than any other culture. The Anglo-American culture also played a major role in the heritage of Appalachia. If you were to take a look at this author's family in Kentucky, you would soon hear stories of the Coat of Arms and the family name. My wife's English heritage took root in this country in 1838, when a twelve year-old boy named Marion came to America. Making his way to Appalachia, he began a tradition of hard work and determination. Many times the only thing a settler to our area possessed was a good name. The English influence is one that prides itself in holding up the good name of the family. This influence is part of our Appalachian culture. In the mountains, a man is only as good as his word, and it is not uncommon for a business agreement to still be sealed with a handshake. I often find myself reminding my own children: "Don't forget whose child you are!" A good family name is something we value and want to pass on to future generations. Regarding a good reputation, once you lose it, it's gone. In rural Appalachia, everyone knows everyone and the value of upholding the family name is a badge of honor! Every person plays their role in the social make-up of a rural Appalachian community,

The First Anglo-Americans to the American Colonies were the Pilgrims, and their story begins in the small north Nottinghamshire village of Scrooby England. Around 1606, a small cluster of religiously devout "rebels of the church" known as Pilgrims chose to form their own church separate from the national Church of England and its King James I. Historically, there were four men who came to the forefront as strong religious leaders of this Pilgrim movement. They were William Brewster, Richard Clifton, William Bradford and John Robinson who stayed in Holland to minister. Their goal: to take a strong stand for church reform in light of their own view of Christian faith and practice. At the time, that was an impossible task in the King's established Church. They were strongly convicted in conscience to begin a church of their own and that meant the establishment of a new covenant (Taylor, 1998). That covenant known as the Mayflower compact, or agreement for self-government, was the cornerstone of our republic and the blueprint of our Constitution. They sought a governing document to guide them in their new life and from this "religious document" a political guide developed. If you look at the who, what, where, when and why of the pilgrims venture into self-determination, you will find that their covenants are foundations for our Constitution and the Declaration of Independence which promote that our civil liberties and political power came from God (Gibbs, 2003).

Because the church and state were almost synonymous, the Church of England looked at their stand as treason. Marked for Treason? Yes, and proud they were for their "separatist" ideas paved the way for other protestant believers to come to the new world. They believed people should have the freedom to worship as they chose. They couldn't stand idle and allow a King to dictate how they should worship. Willing to accept the label "Separatist", they were soon forced to flee the country for fear of imprisonment and execution for their beliefs. They first fled to a secluded area known as Boston in Lincolnshire. Their seclusion didn't last long, for they were soon found and many were placed in prison for their faith. Their next refuge was a little town called Immingham, on the Humber River.

This small cluster of Separatists quickly emigrated in 1609 to safety in the Netherlands. From the Netherlands, they moved to Holland to make a new home. For a while, there was freedom from oppression in Amsterdam. Little by little, problems grew between them and other English religious zealots that had immigrated to Holland. As fate would have it, they turned their sites to America. They left Holland just one year before the truce ended between Holland and Spain in 1621. As they left for the new world, their first goal was to settle the Northern boundaries of land owned by the Virginia Company, at the mouth of the Hudson River. A secular party made up of English investors financed the historical voyage to settle in America and thus joined together with the Pilgrims to become partners in the new colony. They bought a small ship in Holland, called the Speedwell, to make their trip back to England. They sailed to England in the summer of 1620 and there joined a bigger hired vessel called the Mayflower. The rest is history!

The Puritans, who later came to the new world, had a much different approach. Although we often think synonymously of the Pilgrims and Puritans, they did differ in their beliefs and approach to "religious freedom". While the Pilgrims believed Church reform was a waste of time, the Puritans believed they could reform the Church of England from inside. Obtaining "permission" from the King of England, the Puritans brought their best and brightest to the new world to eventually establish a new American legacy. Little did England know that allowing them to elect their own leaders and establish their own laws was only a foreshadowing of self-government as we know it in our own Constitution and Declarations.

Who were these English immigrants known as Pilgrims? Traditionally, we think of them in our annual stories of Thanksgiving. The meals with Indians, strange dresses and unique hats have become a recognizable part of American History. Just like many of the characters of the Bible, we have the tendency to mark them as fictional, but they were real. Who were they? They were a people with a determined spirit. They were you and I.

"Like the early English immigrants, we all carry within us the desire to be self-determined with the right to self-govern our way of life. The Social Work Creed has within it a premise that calls for every individual's right to strive for self-determination."

These religious zealots made a courageous trip to a new world to make their mark in history and claim their self-determination. In doing so, they founded the first New England colony. The English dream was to be free from the hardships of English and Holland rule. They had a new vision: "Freedom in America". They welcomed the name Separatist, for their cry was for all men of English blood to separate themselves from the Church of England and spread their wings of religious freedom. Some of those early New England settlers did not follow that strong pull of religious separation nor were they all die-in-the-wool religious zealots. Their goal in the new world wasn't to seek religious freedom, but economic gains. Whatever their reasoning for coming to America, most of them shared a strong Protestant belief system. That belief system affected every facet of their life (Phillips, 2000). The English brought with them a vivid and colorful culture. Their secular approach to life was strong with educational values and pursuits. A great knowledge of medicine, science, literature, and the strong practice of passing on folk tales and traditions added a wonderful flavor to our culture and their new world became one where education flourished. What appealed to our Anglo-American ancestors? It was the dream of creating a new English society. The best of two worlds meant that they could exercise both religious and economic freedoms in America. A historical timeline of the English is available in Appendix C.

The Swedes in Appalachia: A review of Swedish emigration to early America

The Swedish immigration to America took place long before the States were united. There was not a huge surge of Swedish settlers who came to the Appalachian area, but there were subtle impacts upon our mountain culture. The "jewels" for Appalachia from Swedish values and beliefs were the influence and impact of social group and family. The Swedes made a major impact on the social climate in early America. Strong within it's culture lay a tightly knit core of family and community. True today as in yesteryear, Appalachia is ablaze with that same strong tradition. Wrapped within this same idea and the purpose for the inclusion of the Swedish culture in the legacy of our region is their strong tie to the Lutheran Church. This denomination was a dominant influence in early America and Appalachia. The Lutheran faith also promoted a strong family value system and sense of group that is akin to the spirit of the Appalachian people. It is for these reasons we present a brief history of Swedish immigration to America (Lindberg, 1971). The Swedes started their journey to America around 1638. Unlike the Pilgrims, the Swedes were not mainly religious zealots. There was some religious persecution in their homeland, but the Stockholm Government was the entity that first sent them to North America. Their goal was to establish a colony under the Swedish crown in Delaware. The colony of New Sweden was short lived, for it ended in 1655 when the colony was taken over by the Dutch. Many of the original settlers remained in the colony and kept their strong Swedish presence alive, while others made their way into the South and the fertile Appalachian lands. What other contributions did the Swedes make? Many of the descendants of the Delaware Swedes became outstanding soldiers in the American fight for freedom in the war against England in 1776 (Furer, 1972).

"One of the historical facts uncovered while working on this book was the existence of a predecessor to George Washington as our first president."

You will find this fact interesting if you research the whole story. The predecessor to George Washington was a Swede named John Hanson from Delaware. In 1781, he was elected President of the United States in Congress Assembled. This appointment preceded George Washington as the highest office holder of the new developing nation. The largest record of Swedish immigrants is recorded in the mid 1840s. Most were destined for the industrial job market in New York, while on the flip side a good number of Swedish farmers came to America looking to build farms on the fertile soils of Iowa and Illinois. The farming land found in Appalachia was tantalizing to the Swedish farmers. Still today you will find many of Swedish decent still living in the foothills of the Appalachian Mountains in very small, yet tightly knit communities. Though the strongest hold of Swedes was in Delaware and the New England states, small farming communities of Swedish families began to dot the fresh Appalachian territory. Why did they come? An agricultural crisis in Sweden sent many families looking for a better home. Like other migrations to America, the issues that moved the masses to this new land included economic depression, social crisis, political turmoil and religious strife. Some of these crisis concerns arose out of traditional practices of their culture. One such "tradition" led to overcrowded farmland and became a major influence on Swedish immigration. The tradition in their homeland for large family farms was to divide their land into smaller plots for their children. With each generation, family farms became smaller and unable to sustain a growing population. Family after family became landlocked and ultimately were forced to give up on farming. Their only option was to move into the city to work at non-farming labor. The consequence was an overflowing population of unemployed masses. The population of some Swedish parishes doubled three times over because of this social dilemma. So the emigration to a land of promise was a longed for solution.

"Traditions sometimes create social dilemma. Many times we don't think about the longitudinal dilemmas of traditional practices. We do not think of the consequences and outcomes that are passed on from one generation to another when we hold to social practices that we are unwilling to change."

There was some religious persecution taking place in Sweden, so a "new land" was also tempting for those who wanted the freedom to worship without the pressure of the State Church. The government of Sweden was connected to the State Lutheran Church, and much like England, people who practiced another religion faced persecution. Some areas of Sweden levied fines and jail sentences for those who opposed the State Church. The persecution and prejudice for those of different faiths continued within parts of the nation, and because of this intolerance, another wave of Swedes left the country between 1840 and 1860 on a journey to America. One important social factor for migration from Sweden was a mandatory military service required by the Government. Much like later years in the United States, conscientious objectors fled the country to escape service to the Swedish Government. Young men were required to train in the Swedish military for 30 days out of each year. When the mandatory training reached over 200 days, many young Swedes decided to leave the country rather than face mandatory service in the armed forces (McGill, 1988).

Whether the Swedes had problems with the government, debt, increasing population, lack of land, religious persecution, required military training, lack of social mobility or political objections, they sought out new lives in the United States. Fuel was added to the fire at the end of the 1860s, when Sweden was hit with major famine. Swedish history records three consecutive years of tragedy. The first year of tragedy was 1866. It was a year full of excessive rain and a persistent wet climate that caused agricultural nightmares and the nation's grain fields to rot. The next year, 1867, was just the opposite where the sun and lack of rain caused the crops to burn and dry out in the fields. Finally, the year 1868 saw severe health epidemics and starvation. During these three tragic years, sixty thousand people left Sweden. These tragedies in Sweden influenced steady migration to America that continued strong until World War I. During the years 1868-1914, more than a million Swedes emigrated away from their home country. The emigration resumed after the war, but not on the scale seen in the 1800's. By 1910 there were 1.4 million first and second-generation Swedish immigrants listed as living in the U.S. As mentioned before, one of the strong contributions to our society by the Swedish settlers was their sense of community and group loyalty.

A unique social factor about the Swedish community is that all men did not go off to work each day. It was common in their settlements for one of the men to stay at home to guard and protect while the others worked. In this new land, it seemed almost necessary to stay together for survival. In Appalachia, the rich Swedish traditions of powerful communities and strong group loyalty are practiced from the highest peak to the lowest hollow. Dotted in the hills of Appalachia, you will still find communities of Swedish decent meeting to celebrate a culture that holds strong to their identity (Lindberg, 1971).

> *"Any culture who seeks to retain their individuality and identity as a people show that they live with a strong integrity of purpose. The Appalachian people are such a culture."*

The Irish in a new found land: our Celtic roots in Appalachia

You will find the Irish Immigration and influence in Appalachia covered in many of our history books. Their influence on every part of American history is great and no area of American culture has missed out. The very short history of migration of nations covered in this book will quickly show that the Irish had a profoundly great influence on Appalachian culture.

> *"Like the American Indian, they have suffered loss of their ancestral land; like the blacks, they have endured bondage; like the Jews, they have tasted religious persecution; like the Asians, they have been scorned because they looked and acted "different"; like the Italians and the Slavs, they have been despised as "poor and ignorant"; like the Hispanics, they have been denounced as violent and disruptive." (Griffin, 1998).*

The Irish are famous for passing down stories from generation to generation and old folk tales told in Ireland speak about mysterious lands to the west across the Atlantic. Some historians speculate that a legendary Irishman they called Brendan the Navigator (St. Brendan), wrote that he had found a "Land of Promise and Saints" while on his 7th century voyage in a hide skinned boat. The earliest discovery voyages by Christopher Columbus, and his discovery of America in 1492, included many Irish sailors. To be specific, it is believed a sailor named Galway Ayers (Eris) was on board that first discovery ship. History also records Irish immigrations during the earliest pre-colonial periods of America. They had a strong hand in the discovery and modernization of our new frontiers and have stood toe-to-toe with Americans in war. As people of Irish decent came to America, they made their own unique impression. Some of those who came to America were men and women of Irish noble blood. Others were Irish of common blood that made their living from farming and menial labor. In America, the hard working Irish helped build a strong labor force and were very instrumental in the building of our canals and railroads. Organizing their work force well, they became a strong force in shaping the arts, politics, and work ethic of our early American culture (Foster, 1988).

When the Celtic people settled the Appalachian region, they were not necessarily concerned with expanding their territories. They were worried more about survival and escaping the rule of government, poverty, and religious oppression. Today, in the revival of genealogical searches, many Americans are finding family ties to Irish, Scotch, Scotch-Irish, or Welsh culture. What many do not have is a clear picture of the Celtic world from which they came.

History doesn't go back far enough to tell us who lived on the island of Ireland before the Gaels conquered the natives who lived there. We know that the Danes and Normans of England held control of the island for years. There were many European cultures that intermarried with the Irish, adopted their Irish language, and blended in with the native population. Ireland, like Appalachia, became a blended culture. Most people think of the Irish as having immigrated mainly in the nineteenth century, beginning with the potato famine. In fact, many came much earlier. Irishmen were living in Appalachia before the days of the American Revolution. These Catholic Irish found a difficult problem in their new land. The absence of priests and churches made the active practice of Catholicism impossible in many cases. Rather than abandoning their religious life, many of them became Protestants, Presbyterian, Methodist, and still others joined themselves to Baptist denominations. This is the reason that, to this very day, it is not uncommon in Appalachia to find church rolls including such names as Murphy, Mullins, and O'Brian.

Let's talk history. Historians differ on their recordings of who had the first contact with America. In regard to the Irish, the list of newcomers to America include an Irish crewman named Patrick Maguire, who is said to have accompanied Columbus on his 1492 voyage. Another Irishman already mentioned was William Ayers (or Eris) of Belfast as possibly the first documented American immigrant. Other famous Irishmen were Darbie Glaven and Dennis Carrell, who served as soldiers under Captain John White in Virginia in 1587 (Miller, 1994). Most of our history on mass immigration to America by the Irish focuses on the period of time during the great potato famine of the 1840's, but there was a large group of Irish in America before the famine period. The Irish and Scotch-Irish were part of a steady flow of new settlers in the Appalachian foothills. The Scotch Irish are often referred to as those Scotch-Irish Presbyterians who came from Scotland. They settled in Northern Ireland in the seventeenth century, and then immigrated to the Americas before the American Revolution (O'Grada, 1995).

"They all came here looking for peace. Had they found it? Unfortunately, no! Upon making it safely to America, these new settlers were faced with a cultural dilemma not unfamiliar. They were now in a country full of the English from whom they sought freedom."

As with many new cultures in America, there were conflicts in the early settlements. Because the Irish, Scotch Irish and English clashed in their homelands, it was inevitable that their differences would follow them to the new world. Three of the early colonies (South Carolina, Virginia and Maryland) passed laws limiting the number of servants of Irish and Scotch-Irish decent allowed in their "English" colonies. Included in their acts of prejudice, the Northern colonies pushed to "protect" themselves from the rising general population of Irish and Scotch-Irish settlers. In the Southern colonies, concerns rose over the influx of former servants into the territory. Although those in America were themselves attempting to escape English rule, times of tension still brewed among the mixed cultures of our land. The first Irish and Scotch Irish chose to settle mainly in the Pennsylvania area because of its less restrictive land laws. One of the major benefits of living around the grand city of Philadelphia, PA was its main port of trade and business. However, the push in industry also brought large numbers of Irish and Scotch Irish who willingly came to the Americas to work and live as indentured servants. Those seeking a better life in America met with hard times and harsh urban conditions. The ships coming to America were overcrowded and under-provisioned. Much like today's "boat people", our history tells its own tragedies on the seas.

One of the historical events in Ireland in the latter 1700's was the collapse of its largest industries. The Ulster linen industry was the "bread and butter" of these craftsmen. After its collapse in 1771-72, a large number of Irish came to America looking for a way to make life better. Some historical figures who came from that era were men like Charles Thompson (1729-1824) who came from Londonderry as a young man. He carved out his niche in business and politics, serving as the Secretary of the Continental Congress from 1774 to 1789 (Golway and Coffey, 1997).

It was from their roots in Pennsylvania that the Irish and Scotch Irish began to move south into the Appalachian colonies. The route taken by many of these new Americans was called the Great Philadelphia Road. The road made it's way down the western part of Maryland, south through Virginia's Shenandoah Valley, across North Carolina's central plateau and into mid-South Carolina. This prime Appalachian territory was fertile and ready for farming just as in their homeland. In the later 1740s, Irish and Scotch Irish Americans began to move further South into the Western part of Virginia and on into Kentucky. Although they suffered much in their home country, the life and culture of the Irish survived the tempest. Appalachia was touched by a culture that would firmly transplant itself into Appalachia. Mostly a rural people, they were prime candidates for planting their cultural roots in the fertile mountains. Their Irish migration from across the sea would change and transform America profoundly. Why? The Irish brought with them a proud tradition full of hopes and dreams. A historical timeline is available in Appendix D for a more in-depth study.

"The Irish and Scotch-Irish have influenced our Appalachian culture with art, music, and a strong work ethic. If we go no further in our study, we do know one thing—Our Appalachian culture has been truly enriched."

The Germans in Appalachia: a merging migration to the mountains

What were the reasons for German Emigration? Across the Atlantic Ocean, and covering a large part of central Europe, is a country dear to all Americans of German ancestry. It is known as a land of beautiful scenery and winding rivers that make their way through the highland mountains. The autumn leaves change the colors of the hillsides with outstanding diversity. The foothills are dotted with old community churches sporting quaint steeples and crosses.

"The old brick homes, woods, and hollows are home to old mountain legends and folk tales. If you didn't know better, you might think we were talking about Appalachian lands, but Germany is our topic."

Germany is noted as the home of science and the birthplace of world famous philosophers, poets, artists, sculptors and composers. Americans of German origin cherish it as the land of their forefathers, and lovingly refer to it as the "Old Fatherland". During the middle ages, Germany was a most prosperous and powerful empire in Europe. Villages and cities grew prosperously, and trade and commerce sprang into existence. Germany is famous for its craftsmen who formed powerful guilds within its society and built strong commercial ties with other European countries and nations in the Orient. Germans are a proud people. They took pride in their communities. The proof lies in the fact that their cities and towns "sparkled" with beautiful hand crafted woodwork and finery. They prided themselves in community involvement by giving freely of their skills to make their communities beautiful. Within German cities, the magistrates almost made it a "keep up with the Jones'" affair to beautify their cities. To "put on the Ritz", each city attempted to show their importance and wealth by adorning the entrance gates to towns with decorations of beautiful sculptured work and exquisite carvings in wood. In the middle of public squares, and in front of city halls, were beautiful fountains topped with the figures of famous people, knights or kings. Their homes held hand carved objects such as weather vanes and door knockers done by hand skilled craftsmen. German history also records a period in which great poets, artists, inventors and reformers flourished. Famous Germans included: Berthold Schwarz who invented gunpowder; Johannes Gutenberg who invented movable type; Astronomers Kopernikus and Kepler were some of the first to support the theory that the sun does not move around the earth, but the earth and other planets revolve around it.

In the world of religion, German Martin Luther gave to his people the Bible in their own language and courage to read and write in a literary language. In view of all these facts we may well ask, why did people abandon such a glorious land and immigrate to far distant countries of which they knew nothing and where their future was uncertain? Why did they come to America? The answer is the Reformation. Martin Luther's influence was grand upon many of our German ancestors who came to America. The Reformation was followed by the most overwhelming battles that have plagued a country. Beginning in 1618 and lasting until 1648, the Thirty Years' War blew through Germany like a hurricane. It changed the face of a great country forever (Rabb, 1964). Hundreds of cities and villages were burned during the war. The Spanish, Italian, Hungarian, Dutch and Swedish nations found a battle zone in the lands of Germany. Out of the 17 million citizens of Germany, 13 millions were killed or starved to death in the 30 years of mayhem. The agriculture, trade, industry and art of a great nation were destroyed. Many of the villages and towns were flattened with nothing remaining but ash. Because of their great suffering, many of the people of Germany gave up their dream of a strong homeland and others were stirred with hope.

> "In those years of devastation, a new dream was born of a future in America and a land to call their own. They hoped to enjoy a better life and the freedom to worship in the mountains of a new world."

The German people had learned that William Penn had opened his tracts of land in Pennsylvania for those who would come to America. They prayed it would be a place of refuge to those who suffered persecution for their religious faith. This was one of the main attractions for many Germans to migrate to Pennsylvania in the New World. Some have called them the religious predecessors of the Puritans. Long before the Puritans thought of migrating to America, Germans had already landed in several parts of the New World. Among them were mechanics, artisans, traders and miners who used their skills in the new world to make a living for them and their families (Furer, 1973).

At Plymouth Rock our nation remembers the Pilgrim settlers who braved the new world. In Germantown, we remember German Mennonites who arrived in Philadelphia and then broke ground for the first permanent German settlement in North America. Like the Pilgrims, the Mennonites had been subjected to excessive religious restrictions and persecution and therefore jumped at the chance to come to America (Galicich, 1989).

When slavery became a practice in many of the Appalachian regions of America, the Germans were among the very few to take a public stand. Slaves were sold commonly within the English colonies without even the slightest protest from the Puritans and Quakers. Although they claimed to be strong defenders of human rights, they did not stand up on the slavery issue in the new world. The Germans felt differently because they themselves had suffered so much at home in their own land. They could not keep silent about slavery. Their stand was a fundamental of faith, which they believed was supported by the teachings of Christ. On February 18, 1688 they wrote a protest against slavery. It was the first known public document to have been written on the subject in this era. This document is a little lengthy, but well worth the read.

The German declaration on civil rights for blacks in America

Francis Daniel Pastorius drew up this document. In addition, the German Salzburgers of Georgia, the Germans of the Valley of Virginia, and the Moravians of North Carolina resisted the keeping of slaves as long as was possible. This is the document:

"This is to ye Monthly Meeting held at Richard Warrel's. These are the reasons why we are against the traffick of men Body, as followeth: Is there any that would be done or handled at this manner? To be sold or made a slave for all the time of his life? How fearfull and fainthearted are many on sea when they see a strange vessel, being afraid it should be a Turk, and they should be taken and sold for slaves into Turckey. Now what is this better done as Turcks doe? Yea rather is it worse for them, which say they are Christians; for we hear that ye most part of such Negers are brought hither against their will and consent; and that many of them are nowle. Now, tho' they are black, we cannot conceive there is more liberty to have them slaves, as it is to have other white ones. There is a saying, that we shall doe to all men, like as we will be done our selves; making no difference of what generation, descent or colour they are. And those who steal or robb men, and those who buy or purchase them, are they not all alike?

Here is liberty of conscience, which is right and reasonable; here ought to be likewise liberty of ye body, except of evildoers, which is another case. But to bring men hither, or to robb and sell them against their will, we stand against. In Europe there are many oppressed for conscience sake; and here there are those oppressed, which are of a black colour. And we, who know that men must not commit adultery, some doe commit adultery in others, separating wifes from their husbands and giving them to others; and some sell the children of those poor creatures to other men. Oh! Doe consider well this things, you who doe it; if you would be done at this manner? And if it is done according to Christianity? You surpass Holland and Germany in this thing. This makes an ill report in all those countries of Europe, where they hear off, that ye Quackers doe here nowle men like they nowle there ye cattel. And for that reason some have no mind or inclination to come hither, and who shall maintains this your cause or plaid for it? Truly we can not do so, except you shall inform us better nowle, that Christians have liberty to practise this things. Pray!

What thing on the world can be done worse towards us, then if men should robb or steal us away, and sell us for slaves to strange countries, separating housbands from their wifes and children. Being now this is not done at that manner, we will be done at, therefore we contradict and are against this traffick of menbody. And we who profess that it is not lawful to steal, must likewise avoid to purchase such things as are nowle but rather help to stop this robbing and stealing if possible; and such men ought to be delivered out of ye hands of ye Robbers and sett free as well as in Europe. Then is Pennsylvania to have a good report, instead it hath now a bad one for this sacke in other countries. Especially whereas ye Europeans are desirous to know in what manner ye Quackers doe rule in their

Province; and most of them doe look upon us with an envious eye. But if this is done well, what shall
we say is done evill?
If once these slaves (which they say are so wicked and stubborn men) should joint themselves, fight
for their freedom and nowle their masters and mastrisses as they did nowle them before, will these
masters and mastrisses tacke the sword at hand and warr against these poor slaves, like we are able to
believe, some will not refuse to doe? Or have these Negers not as much right to fight for their freedom,
as you have to keep them slaves?
Now consider well this thing, if it is good or bad? And in case you find it to be good to nowle these
blacks at that manner, we desire and require you hereby lovingly, that you may inform us here in,
which at this time never was done, that Christians have such a liberty to do so, to the end we shall be
satisfied in this point, and satisfie lickewise our good friends and acquaintances in our natif country,
to whose it is a terrour or fairfull thing that men should be handeld so in Pennsilvania.
This is from our Meeting at Germantown held ye 18. of the 2. month 1688. to be delivered to the
monthly meeting at Richard Warrel's. This document was signed by Gerret hendericks, derick op de
graeff, Francis daniell Pastorius and Abraham up Den graeff." (Hendricks, Graeff, Pastorius and
Graeff, 1688)

The German Mennonites strongly proclaimed this stand against slavery and read this
document at church gatherings and public meetings. They presented this document on
slavery at many of the meetings of the Quakers. Their document soon got the Quakers
thinking, because later in 1711, the Quakers introduced their own version entitled: "An
act to prevent the importation of Negroes and Indians into the province". Germany's loss
was America's gain for they brought a sense of conscience concerning the moral and social
issues surrounding civil rights. Their stand on slavery was the first of many 'in your face'
approaches to the subject in the Appalachian territories.

While the first of German immigrants consisted essentially of farmers, general laborers
and traders, there was a second great influx of scholars and students of every branch of
science, art, journalism, law, ministry, teaching and forestry. The great amount of knowledge
and idealism brought to our region by the Germans made them quite valuable to Appalachia.
What value did they bring? Our German American ancestors became our teachers and
professors in American schools and Universities. They filled public offices and started large
newspaper and periodical businesses. These true Americans influenced the face of America
and Appalachia greatly (Furer, 1973). Scattered across the Appalachian Mountains you will
still find small Mennonite towns. The local agricultural agents here in Kentucky work
closely with German Mennonite families who have strong working farms and raising cattle
to etch out a living in a modern society. Several of the wonderful Appalachian treats still
common are the taste of breads and candies. If you happen across their quality quilt work,
crafts and art you have a treat in store. Still today you can travel through many of the small
towns of Appalachia, and much like Germany, you will see city squares, artwork and fancy
architecture on "small town" buildings. Just as in Germany, every little community has its
own small town festivals that are a staple event throughout Appalachia. A historical timeline
of our German ancestors is available in Appendix E and will give you more insight into this
culture that shaped Appalachia. The spirits of sharing and altruistic acts of kindness are
strong German qualities, a sort of community bond. In Appalachia, we still hold that same
spirit and altruistic nature valuable.

"Altruism is entrenched in our Appalachian heritage. It is strong in our nature to give back to the
community of our time, talents and pride. This is Appalachia."

What drew all of our ancestors to the mountains?

I called it a mysterious pull, but the mountains of Appalachia are among the most beautiful in the world. Their forests and hills have been the home of the American native for centuries far beyond "new comers" to America. Our mountains host high and misty peeks, leading to long and hollow valleys like the countryside's of England. Like Sweden's coasts, the coast of New England is home to fishing and trade much like their home. Much like the highlands of Scotland, the Appalachian Mountains stand majestically proud. The Shorelines of the Eastern Appalachian states are dotted with wondrous rocky knolls and ocean spray, much like those on the coasts of Ireland. In some areas they open up to broad valleys with clear mountain streams and waterfalls that dot the land like the beautiful Rhine River of Germany. The tall and towering trees and endless forests provided resources beyond the early mountaineer's dreams. Wild game roamed free in the mountains and foothills. Roots, berries, and medicine herbs grew plenteous and were freely available to early settlers in our mountains. For those coming into Appalachia, it was a place to escape. Escape what? They sought escape from the infringements of government, the demands of the Church and any other "power" that would tell them how to rule their own lives. Reflecting on our statements about their desire for solitude, you can see how the Appalachian Mountains and foothills provided new opportunities and freedoms not known in their homelands. They found freedom from economic restraints and religious controls. They longed for the ability to just "do what they pleased, the way they pleased". In simple terms, solitude!!! These reasons and more are what brought our ancestors to Appalachia. Regardless of their reasons, I am glad they came! The bottom line is this:

> *"The Appalachian people are a perfect image of this Multi-cultural Heritage we call the 'Crayon Box of A Nation'. Through centuries of American history, the lifestyle of the solitude mountain family has taken on a character of its own. Their search for solitude has been misunderstood. It has been "cartooned" by a society who sees the rural mountain family from the viewpoint of a 'cultured society'."*

CHAPTER FOUR

❧

RELIGION IN APPALACHIA:

A culture shaped by their belief

❧

You may ask the question: "What does religion have to do with the shaping of Appalachian culture?" Religion has shaped culture since the dawn of time. To understand the religions and denominational beliefs that shape a great culture is a key to social work practice. So <u>who</u> is the focus of religious faith? <u>What</u> is it that brings people to a given belief? <u>Where</u> did all these denominational beliefs come from? <u>When</u> and <u>why</u> did our ancestors join themselves to a particular faith and practice here in the churches of Appalachia? <u>How</u> did these church ties mold the culture and set ablaze this crayon box of religion we now know in APPALACHIA? Read on and you will find the foundations of our faith.

The Appalachian people are very religious oriented. There are more "religious" people who claim to be of the Christian faith in our country than there are people who practice their faith on any given Sunday. The people of the Appalachian region, as a whole, will claim that their values and meaning in life spring from the Word of God and the influence of the Judeo-Christian ethic. We hold strong to the belief that salvation is by grace through faith. It is that belief and trust that gives the common man a personal relationship with Jesus Christ. This was the driving influence of the Protestant Reformation movement. When Martin Luther nailed his 95 Thesis to the church doors, he was taking a stand for religious freedom for the common man. That same premise of religious freedom is the foundation of our great nation today. Although our nation gives freedom of practice to every religion of the world, our founding fathers came with the strong belief in One God. Simply pick up a coin or dollar bill and you will find in whom we trust.

"The culture in Appalachia is rich with faith and a religious zeal that is the influence of generation after generation of mountain family."

There were many religious denominations in the early years of Appalachia who felt a strong pull to reach the whole "flock" on the frontiers. They met with some of the same challenges on the spiritual level as social workers have on a social level. They did not set out to establish great churches, but to establish many small mission works across the mountains. Their first obstacle was the rural setting. Frontier families were spread out into every hollow, valley, and mountaintop. Since the larger denominations could not reach every family, local autonomous groups sprang up in many of the isolated areas of the mountains. Denominations of many creeds, classes and culture began to appear throughout the mountains of Appalachian.

Do you got religion?

If the topic of religion comes up in a conversation, one might hear: "I'm not a church-goer, but I'm a God fearing person". Having served within the realm of the church for over 30 years, I can attest to the fact that there are a lot of "religious" influences within the lives of even non-churched individuals. Many of the values they live by are passed down from generation to generation. The greatest influence, however, is the influence of those practicing their faith and actively living their faith. Within the realm of the church, individuals develop a social structure that creates a strong support system.

"The church often becomes a surrogate family for those who have no family. Faith becomes the stabilizing factor for those who have no stability in their life."

One of the greatest assets to any social worker working in the Appalachian area is to understand what shapes their faith, beliefs and values. This chapter is a little detailed, but not as detailed as the hundreds of books that cover the topic of origins of religion. I believe it is important for social workers to have a working knowledge of the forces that drive social behavior. The church is one of the strongest influences for the molding of human behavior that I know. For those who may have strong ties to a church or for those who have no ties to a church, this brief peek at the religious roots of Appalachia will be of value as you serve a culture ablaze with religious zeal. It is a short summary of some (not all) of the denominations and faiths that shape our personal experiences in Appalachia. Although this is not an all-inclusive study, I will try to cover such influential beliefs and churches as the Anglican, Episcopal, Catholic, Puritan Separatist, the Protestant Movement, Presbyterian, Lutheran, Quaker/Shaker, the Anabaptist Movement, Baptist, Mennonite, Amish, Brethren, Methodist and the Restoration Movement. Knowing the religious backgrounds that influence any culture will allow social workers to gain a greater knowledge of how organized religion influences personal experience, lifestyle and attempts to deal with social dilemma. Learning about the history of religious denominations in Appalachia is as important as knowing the national origins of our culture. As we take a look at church history from the early years of America, we will see how it shaped the social conditions of the people. Just like the cultural heritage of nations helped shape the face of Appalachia, so did religion. This chapter is a look at denominations and how personal "religious" experiences shaped their lives.

"Knowing church history and what the church has to say about social issues will help us understand how to work through the problem solving and planned change process with people in our care."

The Anglican faith

So what is Anglicanism? It is the Church of England. It is the branch of the Christian church that, since the Reformation, has been the established Church of the English. History gives unquestionable evidence of its organization in the 3rd and 4th century. Many denominations claim to have roots in the Church of England including Protestantism, the Methodists, Lutherans, and others that will be spoken of later in this chapter (Holmes, 1982). The Anglican Church can site many of its rituals and disciplines as being influenced by the Celtic and Gallic missionaries and monks who came to England. When St. Augustine and his missionary companions came to England from Rome around 597 A.D., the Celtic influences of worship faded away. The influences of the Romans took over in their forms of worship. During the next four centuries, the church in Saxon England grew and developed much like many of the organized churches of the Middle Ages. After the Norman Conquest (1066), the English church came under the powerful influence of the Roman Catholic Papacy. The authority of Roman Popes, such as those from Gregory VII to Innocent III, held the Church of England tight to the Catholic Church. Several times during the medieval period, English kings tried to pull away from the power of the church. It wasn't until the reign of Henry VIII that a new national "Anglican" church was formed. The acts of Parliament between 1529 and 1536 marked the beginning of the Anglican Church as a national church independent of Papal jurisdiction (Webber, 1999).

At the time, the decision of Henry VIII to secede from the Catholic Church was seen as revolutionary. Whether his reason was purely selfish or not, he received great support from those in England. After Henry's death, the influences of religious reform were felt more strongly in England. In the year 1549, the first Anglican Book of Common Prayer was published. The Church required its clergy to use the book out of an Act of Uniformity for the Church. As the years went on, a second prayer book was published that had a more Protestant flavor. If you were to compare the first book of prayer to the second, you would clearly see that the influence of Protestantism was creeping up in the Church. In 1552, the Forty-two Articles of the Anglican Church were written and adopted and became the Church's new doctrinal statement (Moorman, 1983). When members of the Anglican Church in the first American colonies could no longer give their allegiance to the mother church overseas, a number of autonomous churches were established apart from the Anglican Church in England.

Whichever historical view you take of the Anglican Church, you will find that it is not a strong denomination within America. It did however, have some affect upon our American culture. The Panther and the Hind is a good book to read about Anglican Church history. In its time, it was a controversial book. It does, however, speak of wide differences between branches of the church and their traditions. All of them lay claim to Anglican roots and ties to the Church of England. According to the book, different branches of Anglicanism were in agreement on two things. First, all Anglicans were to be led by the authority of bishops. These bishops held the Anglican Church together socially, and were the final authority within their own dioceses. Secondly, most Anglicans were in agreement with common prayer and worship, which focused around the "Authorized Version of the Bible" and a Common Book of Prayer used in all their worship. Over the years, some of the Anglican Catholics, particularly in England, did not choose to use the prayer book in worship. Other variations within the modern church during the 1970's, such as the ordination of women, even further divided the Anglican Church (Nichols, 1992).

> *"To say that Appalachia was influenced by this rich religious culture is an understatement. The Anglican Church is a "mother" of sorts to diversity in doctrinal belief and freethinking worship."*

Outside of America, the influence of the Anglican Church is strong. It's roots spring to Wales, Ireland, and Scotland (the Episcopal Church). Independent Anglican churches are spread abroad in Canada, Australia, New Zealand, Western Africa, Central Africa, the Republic of South Africa, India, China, Japan and the West Indies. The Anglican Church and its missions are located in nearly every area of the world. People of diversity all over the world have embraced this Anglican belief system and the influence of the Anglo-Saxon culture. They constitute a "communion" bound together by their common faith and practice.

The Episcopal faith

The Episcopal Missionary Church is a traditional Anglican Church that has attempted to keep the apostolic origins and practices of the earliest Christian faith. Where the Anglican and Episcopal Church differ is in what they believe on church rule and the believer's priesthood. There are three important things the Episcopal Church stands for which distinguishes them in their belief. The first is their outlook on the Bible. Their belief was that God and its authors speak directly to us through the Bible. The common man can find all they need there. The second strong belief was their tradition. They claimed that their traditions were those handed down by Jesus himself. Thirdly, they were freethinking. They did not have a set of man-made rules to follow. They promoted that freethinking believers should use their minds to determine their own walk with God.

> *"Doesn't this free-thinking philosophy sound like the premise of self-determination taught under the Code of Ethics for social work? Further study into church polity shows a strong support for general systems theory."*

Those in the Episcopal faith believed a person's focus should be to think about the Bible, tradition and our own experience in ways that bring a goodness of fit. One of the distinguishing traits of the Episcopal Church is the Common Book of Prayer, which guides their standard of faith, practice and worship (Benton, 1975). In church leadership, the decisions in the Episcopal Church are made by a "system" of people elected to represent each individual diocese. Let me share with you how that system is arranged. At the highest level of social "make-up" within the denomination, is one bishop who is the leader of the Episcopal Church. This Bishop leads and serves, but does not control the church. Under the head Bishop are other bishops who lead a small "Diocese" within a geographical area, which might be best illustrated as a state or a county. This Diocese is then divided into smaller parishes or missions. The priest who leads a parish is called the Rector, and a priest who leads a mission is called the Vicar. When it comes to the local church, the people in the congregation serve the parish on a council called a Vestry. In matters of the denomination, there is a National General Convention every three years where elected representatives from each geographical area meet to make decisions for the whole Episcopal Church. From the viewpoint of a social worker, we might well study the church, for its systems do help us define those with whom we most want to affect change (Prichard, 1991).

"What do social work and church polity have in common? A person familiar with generalist practice and social work education may learn much and find that religion often mimics 'systems' theory quite well."

The Pilgrim and the Puritan movement

The first religious influences most Americans think of are the Pilgrim and Puritan Movements and their search for religious freedom. Although we have already discussed the secular influences of these upon Appalachia, please read on as their history is applied to the spiritual influences upon Appalachian culture.

John Robinson, who lived around 1575-1625, was the first pastor of the Pilgrims. Many of his writings survived the years, and give us a clear picture of the Pilgrims religious beliefs and theology. The Separatist movement of the Pilgrims has its roots with John Calvin, and many hold to the belief that from his religious views and influence sprang the doctrinal standards of Puritanism and Presbyterianism. The Pilgrims' have their roots in Nottinghamshire, England. When King James I took the throne in 1607, the persecution of Protestants began to escalate, and followers of the Protestant faith had to begin to meet secretly.

"Persecution and discrimination is as old as history itself, and it is no respecter of persons or religion. The social impact of spiritual persecution is profound upon any culture."

These Protestants were often hunted down and put in prison, simply because the Church of England did not sanction their religious practices. The only recourse for them was to plan their escape to Amsterdam, Holland and later to a place called Leyden. The following is a basic outline of some of the religious beliefs supported and practiced by the Leyden Pilgrims. These doctrinal beliefs definitely influenced their social outlook on life.

The Pilgrims, who followed Calvin, believed that all things are pre-ordained. They had the view that before the foundation of the world, God predestined to make the world, man and all things. He also pre-destined who would become a child of God. Election is the term they used. It states that only those God elected would receive God's grace and eternity. They believed there was nothing an individual could do during their life that would cause them to become a child of God or to be rejected as a child of God. Their life was spent in attempting to determine if they were one of the elect.

There were only two sacraments practiced by the early Pilgrims. Those were baptism and the Lord's Supper. The other church sacraments practiced in the Church of England and the Anglican Church (Confession, Last Rites, Penance, Confirmation, Ordination and even Marriage) were viewed as inventions of men. As far as the pilgrims were concerned, they were not holy or even necessary to practice (Beale, 2000). Further, the Pilgrims adamantly opposed the Mass. All their lives they had been forced to participate in Mass within the church, and so they rejected it greatly. One of their greatest "protests" was that the Pope was their mediator before God. They were apposed to the ideas that men could be appointed as "Saints" and that Church leaders should have complete rule over the common parish. When it came to the inclusion of icons and religious symbols such as crosses, statues, stain-glass windows, fancy architecture and other manifestations of religion in their worship, they were rejected. The religious relics and symbols once held dear in their former church held no special meaning for them any longer. In regard to church organization, the church of the Pilgrims recognized five different church leaders. They were pastor, teacher, elder, deacon and deaconess. It was not unusual for women to hold leadership roles in the church. So flexible were they about their church make-up that they did not consider those positions as necessary for the running of the church. The Pastor was an ordained minister whose responsibility was to see to the religious life of the congregation. The Teacher was also an ordained minister who was responsible for teaching the congregation, especially the children. The Elder was the eyes and ears of the church. This layman helped the Pastor and Teacher in working with the congregation. The Deacon collected offerings and attended to the needs of the poor and elderly. The Deaconess also helped with the sick and poor and often played the role of mid-wife. Often referred to as the "meeting place" or "meeting house", their place of worship was drab and free from religious symbols and tapestry. The church building itself was not a 'sacred place' to the Pilgrims. It was just a building. Their focus was on the worship experience not the worship place (Hulse, 2001).

In regard to the practices within the church, the Pilgrims practiced infant Baptism and also believed baptism to be the act that washed away sin. Believing this wholly, they encouraged the children to be baptized as soon as possible. Infant baptism was a very controversial issue among many of the early churches. These Pilgrims believed that Baptism was essential for salvation and a stamp of God's covenant with man. They did, however, hold that at least one parent must be of the faith before a child could be baptized into the church. The Pilgrims faithfully observed the Sabbath as a Holy day (Holiday). They did not recognize many of the "Religious" Holidays that we do today. To them, Holidays were invented by man and could not be supported by Scripture. The firm belief was that if it wasn't in the scripture, it should not be recognized as a Holy day. These devout believers had a strong belief in the separation of religious and civil matters. So much so, that they considered marriage a civil affair to be handled by public authorities. It was their belief that the church should not be a part of the union of couples, yet they viewed marriage as ordained by God for the benefit of man's natural and spiritual life. Because it was a civil institution, a marriage became a contract, mutually agreed upon by a man and a woman. For its leader, the church did not practice celibacy in the priesthood, as did the Catholic Church from which they came (Hulse, 2001). The Pilgrims were not far from the idea that it takes an entire village to raise a child. They believed in the child's early years a mother was the most important educator. As the child grew, the father became the more important figure for teaching the real lessons of life. Education was valued. However, there were few teachers in the early years of America's Plymouth Colony who were qualified to teach. Young boys were the focus of education rather than the girls. If young girls learned, it was either on their own or in the home.

"Though this practice was unintentional, gender discrimination was clearly practiced in the education of children in the early years of Appalachia. The role of women was one of social responsibility and labor and education took on a secondary role."

What textbook did they use? The Bible. The common man in the English church was encouraged not to read for himself. Especially unheard of in their life in England, was for women and children to read from the Holy Book. Now that they were free to read on their own, it became their textbook for reading, writing and social development. One of the driving forces behind their original "pilgrimage" was this freedom to read and study the Bible in their own common language (Packer, 1990).

The Pilgrims were strong on "discipline". In our society we would look at much of this as abusive, but in their day the rod of correction was applied generously. They practiced corporal punishment and believed the scriptures supported that view. Here is an interesting bit of history on discipline. In any given Pilgrim home, the children were expected to learn that the wife was <u>also</u> to be disciplined by the husband just as the children. Whenever she disobeyed her husband or sinned against God, the husband was to whip the wife as well. I am sure many of us are glad we do not live in a puritan society, but these Pilgrims's distinction between disciplining a wife by whipping and beating a wife was very clear. Community leaders monitored the discipline of children and wives. Abusive treatment of women was not allowed and looked down upon strongly. In their society, abuse happened seldom, but when it did, the civil court administered punishment to the man. As it should, it included a public whipping. They would not put up with abuse in the community. I love one of their practices that carried over into our Appalachian culture. As recent as the 1960's, there was a practice among the mountain people that I wish we could rekindle They had their own way of dealing with a man in the community who beat his wife. When it became common knowledge that a man was beating his wife and children, the men of the community would gather up bundles of switches and put them on the porch of the abuser. The switches served as a warning that the men of the community would come and use the switches on him should he not stop! The influences of the Pilgrims are still strong in Appalachian society. Though we may not call them "Pilgrim" philosophies and outlooks, they are still felt in our culture today.

The Catholic faith

What is "Catholic?" The word "Catholic" is generally synonymous with the word "universal". In the ancient Church, it was used to refer to a single, visible "communion" or congregation, separate from any other denomination (Collinge, 1997). The Roman Catholic Church is currently the largest denomination in the world. However, as we see the history between it and the Anglican Church, its influence decreased over the years in America. Its influence in Wales and Scotland in the nineteenth century slipped as well. We see the same thing with those early settlers who came to America. The Catholic Church was not strong in early America, nor in the Appalachian area. From the time Henry VIII embraced Catholicism as the official Church of England (or Anglican Church), the Catholic Church remained a minority in England. Those Catholics who remained faithful to the Church of Rome, instead of the "English" church, were often looked upon with suspicion (Frank, 1995).

> *"English Catholics suffered persecution and were often denied many civil rights that would include such common rights as owning property, attending some of the finer colleges, serving in Parliament and those basic rights given to 'non-Catholic' citizens."*

Several events happened in the nineteenth-century to change the acceptance of Roman Catholics. First, the English Parliament passed civil rights laws allowing Catholics to serve as English Legislators and gave Irish Catholics more rights under the law. Secondly, Pope Pius IX reorganized the Roman Catholic Church making a historical declaration which declared the words spoken by the Pope to be infallible. This included his messages and pronouncements on moral issues and doctrinal interpretations. It was this declaration that caused many to wander away from the Catholic Church and question the Pope as the leader of the Catholic Church. As Catholics began to pull away from the church at Rome, they began their search for new places to freely practice their faith and worship...such as America (Trevor-Roper, 1984).

Protestantism: The root of many denominations

Protestantism is a generic term meaning "protestors". It was given to any group who protested the rule of the "Official Church" over the spiritual life of the believer. The main individual given credit for spurring on the protestant movement was the German professor-priest Martin Luther. He issued a challenge to the church around 1517 to guard against becoming too involved in politics, wealth and worldly issues. Luther wanted to see the church get back to spirituality, and help the common man understand that they had the same rights and spiritual equality as any Pope or Priest. To make his point clear, he translated the Bible into German for the common people. The Church was appalled at Luther's boldness and ordered him to quit his challenges to church authority. When Luther refused, the protestant movement was born. The movement of "Luther", hence, the Lutheran Church began spreading across Germany, Scandinavia and soon won support in Europe. For the first time, the low and middle class people of Europe could worship with a freedom of conscience. The protestant movement embraced them with open arms and they found solace with the teachings of Martin Luther. It didn't take long for men like Calvin to train Bible scholars and teachers who took the teaching of Protestantism throughout England, Scotland, the Netherlands, France, Germany, Bohemia, Hungary—and even parts of Poland and Spain. One of the final straws that broke the camels back for Luther was a lavish building program at the Saint Peter's Basilica in Rome. For him it was just an example of how the church had embraced the world. In protest, Luther took hammer and nail and placed a written document called the 95 Theses on the door of the Wittenburg castle. One of the main topics was his theological protest of the sale of indulgences to pay for the Pope's private "projects."

Another historical reformer who stirred up protests against the church was John Wycliff (1320-1384). While at the famous Oxford University, Wycliff taught the common people that they had individual freedom to stand before God. He stood firm against many of the rituals practiced in the formal church. It was under the influence of John Wycliff that the Bible became available through an English translation of the Vulgate. To continue efforts to bring the gospel to the common believer in a Catholic world, Wycliff founded a group of untrained preachers called Lollards. They traveled, preached and shared his teachings all over England until the Roman Catholic Church enforced a declaration called the "De Haeretico comburendo" (burning the heretics). This decree passed by the Parliament called for the punishment by death of the Lollards. Even under threat of death, they were never totally eliminated. This persecution prepared the way for a great church reformation in England. The Bohemians, who studied at Oxford University, brought Wycliff's teachings to a new people. It is thought his teachings influenced John Huss' life and the Bohemian Reform (Robertson, 1984).

John Huss (1374-1415) is another name that comes to light when studying great leaders of the protestant reformation. His platform for protest began at the University of Prague. He was so supportive of Wycliff's work that he translated it into his native Czech language. In 1414, Huss was summoned to a council meeting by the official church where the Council of Constance arrested him and burned him at the stake for his heresy (Gillett, 2001).

"The thought of individual religious freedom was foreign to the people. The message of Huss created a fear in the ranks of the official Church."

A young priest named Ulrich Zwingli came to the forefront of the reformation movement in Zurich, Switzerland. He was a contemporary of Martin Luther. Influenced by Luther's teachings, he boldly spoke that the Scripture was to be the only source of authority for the Christian. He and Luther had much in common, but much in contrast. Their differences were over whether to reform or replace the organized Church. Luther agreed with the Episcopal form of church government and Zwingli did not. They also disagreed on the Lord's super. Zwingli interpreted the idea of Christ actually being in the wine and bread as purely symbolic. To Luther, the sacrament of the Lord's super had the power of the real presence of Christ in the elements. From that point, Lutheranism and the Reformed movement split permanently (Gordon, 2002).

Enter the protestant movement in France. Its leader was John Calvin (1509 to 1564). Within the borders of France, his teachings were not well accepted. When Calvin fled France, he took up roots in Geneva, Switzerland where he created a strong movement of Christians who followed his teachings and interpretations of scripture. Geneva became the home of his model Christian city often called the "New Jerusalem" of Protestantism (Wells and Nicole, 1985).

"It is quite apparent that culture is shaped by religion and religion shapes government. By the 1600's it became important for nations and world leaders to line up on one side or another on the issue of the Protestant Reformation."

Whether for political or religious reasons, the wars between Protestants and Catholics raged on. It is also clear, as one looks at history, that "religious" wars between European kings and kingdoms spurred one conflict after another. These wars devastated Europe and changed the face of religion forever. Fed up with the war of beliefs, a group of philosophers introduced a new approach to faith. That approach was man's individual enlightened points of view. Most philosophers did not promote giving up on faith and practice, but there was a great push to make an abrupt departure from the traditional spiritual views of the church. The need for "enlightenment" became the new push in spirituality. Those who had been told what to believe all their life could finally live in a freethinking world. The Enlightenment was not a matter of just leaving religion alone, but of expanding religion with new enlightening revelations from the individual. The belief that developed from this Enlightenment movement was each person's right to claim that they were inspired. At stake here was something bigger than a battle between Catholics and Protestants. This attempt at freethinking religion bread many new denominations whose leaders claimed divine inspiration (Young, 1998).

"The intention of the Enlightenment philosophers was not to do away with Christianity, but to pull the best things out of it and insert each person's own 'enlightenments' as righteous. The real issue was this: Is Christianity really a religion 'inspired' by God or are the truths taught down through the ages the 'enlightened' teachings of mere men?"

The Presbyterian faith

When we talk about Presbyterianism, we look to the churches in England and Scotland who followed the teachings of John Calvin. Presbyterianism consists of a Church system that governs through presbyteries led by ministers and elders. The Presbyterian Church in the United States is often considered to be an offspring of the Church of Scotland. There was not a hierarchy of leaders within the church, and the only offices held in the church were the role of presbyter and elder. They were pretty much equal in their status within the church. The individual Church's group of elders governed the local Presbyterian congregation. The hierarchy of leadership in the denomination was a simple graduation. One group of elders answered to a larger group of elders in the Province, who then looked to a General Assembly of the Church (Boice, 1986). The Church of Scotland ("the Kirk") adopted a fully Presbyterian system of church government as early as 1690. As the 18th century came around, the Presbyterian movement became less and less followers of Calvin's teaching. The movements of the Episcopalians and the remnants of an extreme Presbyterian movement were on the rise. The first Presbytery of the United States was formed about the year 1700. To have money enough to support the church and its missionary work, the Presbytery and the old Synod called for annual collections from all their churches.

"The money was sent to support mission work in the mountains and poor settlements on the new frontier. Many of these were in the Appalachian region."

As these territories grew, so did the vision to take "the church" to the "ends of the earth". Mountain missions became the new vision of the church. So strong was their vision for missions, they formed a committee on missions in 1802, and organized one of the first Boards of Missions in our country. They have been an example for other denominations ever since. Their zeal to reach and preach the Word of God was further proven by their mass distribution of Bibles to our early Appalachian settlements (Smith, 1985).

The Lutheran faith

History shows that the first Lutheran ministries in the New World were those that targeted mission work. The New Sweden settlement in the Delaware River Valley was a strong new home for both Swedish and Finnish Lutherans. Some of the early colonists formed Lutheran Congregations, while others joined the established Episcopal Church on their arrival in America.

Jacob Fabritius was one Lutheran missionary who came from the Netherlands to America to work with the American Indians. His outreach to them was one of the first efforts to share the beliefs of the Lutheran Church in the new world. Another figure in Lutheran history was Rasmus Jensen. He was one of many Lutheran missionaries, but was actually the first Lutheran pastor in the New World (Lutz, 1985).

John Campanius, referred to as the "saintly apostle of the Indians", was called to pastor the congregation of the first Swedish settlement in North America. His burden for missions was to reach out to the Delaware Indians. The zeal of John Campanius led him to translate some of Martin Luther's small catechisms into the Delaware language. He is also given credit for building the first Lutheran church building in America.

Another historical figure of Lutheran faith was John Conrad Weiser Jr. His efforts to further the Lutheran faith and reach the First Nations people were more successful than his predecessor. He chose to live with the Maqua tribe for close to eight months, learning their language and customs. Looking at examples of true evangelism, I believe he was a missionary in the true sense of the word. The Maqua culture adopted him into their tribe and both the American Indians and European government held this Lutheran missionary in high respect. He was a strong advocate for peace during the French and Indian War (ELCA, 2002).

Justus Falckner was a German immigrant who came to North America in 1700 as an attorney and surveyor of land. His faith compelled him to build relationships with the Swedish and Dutch missionaries, and he soon became an active part of the Dutch Lutheran congregation of New York. He was ordained there as a minister and began to make his mark on the new world church. Diversity in worship was the focus of this minister's outreach. His parish was an example of the crayon box of colors in a growing new world. Like all of Appalachia, his church was composed of a mixture of Dutch, German, African Americans, and American Indians (ELCA, 2002).

The Appalachian South owes much of its Lutheran History to John Bachman. He was the strong leader of St. John Lutheran Church in Charleston, South Carolina. Bachman was one of the first to cross the racial boundaries and reach out to African Americans. In one year, he baptized 90 African American converts to the Lutheran faith. His congregation was up to 40 percent African American before the Civil War. Although he owned slaves and believed in the Confederacy, he still had some vision. He desired to share the gospel and provide an education to African Americans. It was a statement of defiance to offer education to blacks during that time, and illegal in the South. Bachman didn't care about the rule of the time. His push for human rights and equality is evidenced by the notoriety of several African American churchmen in early American history. Among those was Jehu Jones the first African American ordained by American Lutherans. Daniel Alexander Payne became the founder and president of Wilberforce University, Drayton Boston University and the first black missionary to go back to Africa. The Lutheran faith had much to contribute to early America and our multi-cultural roots in Appalachia (ELCA, 2002).

Quakers and Shakers

The Quaker Religious group came to America from England in the mid 1600's. George Fox was their English founder and in the seventeenth century they called themselves the "Society of Friends". They do not call themselves a congregation. They use the term "a meeting". Quakers became so prevalent in the late 1600s that a natural progression was to have annual meetings. They formed themselves into a confederation of regional "meetings". They had hoped to find religious freedom in the colonies, but the very ones who came here to escape persecution (the Puritan settlers) alienated the Quakers. They left Plymouth and settled in the New Bedford area, which they called Dartmouth (Cooper, 1990). When we think of the Quakers, we often think of them as a passive culture, having nothing to do with society. However in England, they were considered a radical Protestant group. They came into the public eye during the English revolution as a people strongly opposed to war. Taking a silent yet public stand on issues was common for the Society of Friends.

I believe an appropriate parallel could be drawn between them and the American pacifists of the 1960's. It is not a far cry to say they were conscientious objectors to the rules of the King and were passive yet bold. In their daily speech, they did and still do practice using the scriptural language of the Bible. Mainly because they felt it kept them close to the Word of God. Their practice of refusal to remove hats inside of a building came from George Fox's stand on never paying reverence or signs of reverence to any man, especially the King. The Quakers view their spiritual life as a completely internal experience. They do not practice any of the familiar church sacraments or outward rituals when they worship. They teach that divine revelation does not come from listening to an ordained minister or from being in the church.

> *"Their religious view is that divine revelation comes from within each person, much like social workers believe self-determination must be internally motivated by an individual."*

The "Quaker" name given to the Society of Friends came about as individuals experienced a "divine revelation" or "inner light" during worship. This experience was often an outward physical shaking or quaking, thus they were given the name Quaker or Shaker. Because they focused on the inner spiritual experience, anyone had the freedom of Spirit to speak in meeting. As any member may be "moved by the Spirit" to witness, all members at a meeting for worship could be inspired to lead the church in worship (Selleck, 1995).

> *"Even women? Yes. It was very unusual, but Quaker women could preach and speak in meeting even in the early days of the denomination. Although they may not consider it so, they were the first religious or civil group to support women's rights."*

In some areas, the Quakers were very quiet and simple. Their clothing was a prime example of simplicity. In other areas they were very outspoken. Quakers were known for their strong rejection of slavery, and their religious views influenced the Northern States to embrace the idea of freeing the slaves. Some believe they helped spur the abolitionist movement in the North. Our Quaker friends had a strong dedication to hard work and helping the community. They were one of the first denominations to focus on ministering to those in poverty. They had a strong kindred spirit to our present day philanthropists. One might even believe they had the heart of social workers (Selleck, 1995).

The Shakers are a splinter group that found root in the Quaker community of Manchester, England. Led by a preacher named James Wardley, the members of this movement followed the teachings of the French reformers. The members of this movement were given the name Shaking Quakers and were considered by many early church leaders as a radical religious group. Why? Mainly because of their attempts to communicate with spirits of the dead and their outward shaking that took place during their services (Stein, 1992). One of the women that came to notoriety in this movement was Ann Lee. She claimed that she experienced a "revelation" while she was in prison for her faith. Lee claimed to be the Second Coming of Christ, the essential female incarnation of God. If you do psychotherapy you might be thinking narcissistic behavior. Lee adopted the title of " God the Father-

Mother" for herself. This vision had by Lee, launched her into the place of "official leader" of the congregation as "Mother" Ann among the Shakers. This radical teaching hurled them into persecution by most every denomination of the day. A small group, made up of her immediate family, began to look toward America as a haven for their religious beliefs. And so they came. They struggled in America with few converts until joined by converts from England who came here with Joseph Meacham. Meacham took over the movement after the death of "Mother" Ann. By the middle 1800's, they hit their height of membership.

The Shakers way of life has become almost a novelty in America with their crafts and community life. From the time the civil war ended and the industrial world exploded with machinery and mass production, their way of life almost disappeared.   Not much is known now of the few 20th Century Shaker communities. Just a few sites remain such as Canterbury, New Hampshire, Sabbath Day Lake, Maine, and two museums in Pleasant Hill, Kentucky and South Union, Kentucky. Near Lexington, Kentucky there is still a "Shaker Town" to visit should you want to learn more (Francis, 2001).

The Anabaptist movement

The term Anabaptist was used to describe and define certain Protestant Christians during the Reformation. These Christians rejected infant baptism, choosing instead to practice believer's baptism. The Anabaptists believed that baptism was simply an initiation ceremony into the church of believers, and should only be administered to believing adults. Since many of them had been baptized in their infancy, they chose to be re-baptized as believing adults. Their "opponents in the faith" called them Anabaptists or "re-baptizers."

The Mennonite (Anabaptist) movement

The Mennonite (Anabaptist) faith movement began in Europe in the 16th Century. Their roots took hold around Zurich, Switzerland. The first church leaders identified with this Swiss movement included men like Menno Simons from whom they adopted their name. They stood strong on the issues of complete separation of Church and State, baptism by confession of faith, nonviolence, nonconformity and piety. They placed their strong stands into the denominations document entitled the "Mennonite Confession of Faith." This Zurich based group and other small groups of Mennonite believers stood in controversy with the reforms of Martin Luther and other reformers during the Protestant Reformation. They were a little more radical than was Luther. Their focus was strong on adult rather than infant baptism. In 1525, a group of "Anabaptists" went public with their views. They pitted themselves against the official church by publicly declaring a faith in Christ and re-baptizing each other (Bowman, 2001).

The official church and state did not stand for this more radical movement of the Anabaptists. These Anabaptists were persecuted harshly and many met death. To keep practicing their faith, the movement went into seclusion. From 1575 to 1850 they were silent and continued only as their faith was passed on to their children. The teaching they passed on to their children included the idea of passiveness. They claim their stand is from Christ's own teachings of peace. Many members refuse or choose not to engage in the military. They take a strong stand against government spending on the military, and others in the group take an even more radical stand by withholding a percentage of their annual income tax as a protest to military spending (Loewen, 1993). A positive quality of the Mennonite movement is their strong commitment to community. On social issues, they are strongly conservative yet proactive in the way they deal with social problems.

"Their altruism is to be admired in society, as their goal is to reach out to communities during loss and disaster. They truly embrace the teaching to feed the hungry, clothe the naked and meet the needs of the helpless."

The Amish (Anabaptist) movement

The Amish trace their history through the Mennonite community. Both were part of the early Anabaptist movement in Europe during the time of the Reformation. A Swiss bishop named Jacob Amman was one of the first who broke from the Mennonite church. His followers still bear his name: "Amish." The Mennonites and Amish have divided several times through the years, but still agree on issues of baptism, non-resistance and basic Bible doctrines. Like the Mennonites, these Amish Anabaptists believed that only adults who had confessed their faith should be baptized and separate themselves to a more isolated life. Both Catholics and Protestants in Europe put many of these Amish Anabaptists to death as heretics. To survive, they fled to the mountains of Switzerland and Southern Germany. It was in the mountains that the Amish tradition of farming and holding their worship services in homes rather than churches began (Hostetler, 1989).

The Amish, like most seeking freedom of worship, migrated to America in search of relief from persecution. But unlike other religious denominations, the Amish had a very strong sense of maintaining their ways. The Amish did not embrace a "new life" in the new world. They held sacred the lifestyle and religion of their ancestry. Around the 1700's, Amish settlers began to make their way to America and form settlements in Southern Pennsylvania. As their numbers grew, they developed strong communities in Ohio, Indiana and Kentucky. During the 19th century, the Amish community experienced social growth, which lead to a new dilemma. They had never developed a universal set of socially accepted practices other than the Bible. What was their solution? They wrote a collection or set of "accepted" rules for behavior within the community called the Ordnung. When they came to America, they experienced some internal divisions over the interpretations of the Ordnung. The Ordnung was not only a written guideline of acceptable social practices, but also one of religious conduct for the Amish. Like most man made denominations, each community of Amish had differing opinions on matters of dress, technology, language, form of worship and interpretation of the Bible. Although the Amish seem stuck in history socially, their way of life is a matter of choice and strong self-determination (Hostetler, 1993).

"They believe strongly in their own autonomy to accept social change or not accept social change. Each church and community decides for itself what it will and will not embrace from society."

The Old Order groups chose to be more primitive and drive horses and buggies rather than cars. Most still have no electricity in the home and send their children to private, one-room schoolhouses. Eighth grade is as far as many children attended school, simply because they held that their children did not need education past this level. Many Mennonites and progressive Amish do make the choice to attend high school and even college today. Yet again, it is a matter of choice and autonomy. It is this choice and a desire for autonomy among Amish communities, which brought about separation between those who chose to be conservative or progressive. The names that identified this division were "Old Order Amish" and "Amish Mennonite". There are still many active Amish communities in Appalachia. A visit to these communities will give anyone a taste of their wonderful culture (Bowman, 2001).

The Baptist Faith

The first Baptists originated from a group of Protestant Christians who believed basically the same doctrines as the 16th-century reformers. Their focus of doctrine was justification by faith, the authority of the Bible, and the priesthood of the believer. If you were to try and draw a distinction between them and other protestant movements it would be their practice of baptism of believers by immersion only. They held strong to the separation of church and state and the autonomy of the local church. These stands are what made the Baptist denomination unique (McBeth, 1990). The Baptists make up almost two-fifths of today's Protestant population. They claim some of the same religious convictions as the Anabaptists, but there is no formal tie to each other. History shows that the Baptist faith began in the early 17th century under the influence of John Smyth and Thomas Helwys in Holland and England. They separated from the Anglican Church as part of the protestant movement with the first recorded Baptist church being founded in Amsterdam around 1609. Taking his faith from Holland to England, Thomas Helwys inspired a small group of Christians to begin the first Baptist church near London. As many denominations do, the English Baptists divided over doctrine and church polity. The General Baptists were Armenian by culture and believed salvation was for 'all' people. The Particular Baptists accepted the views of Calvin and held strong to the doctrine of predestination or election. Eventually, these two groups worked through their differences and came together once again to administer an effective missionary program. From their English roots, the Baptist faith has grown to over 1 million members in Europe.

Baptists in America experienced great growth under the leadership of Roger Williams. He was the pastor and founder of the first Baptist church in America at Providence, Rhode Island. Newport, Rhode Island was the site of another strong Baptist congregation lead by Doctor and Pastor John Clarke. During the early years of the denomination, the Baptists were the objects of some bitterness from other reformed denominations until the period of the Great Awakening (Russell, 1976). Church history shows the Baptists were great supporters of the fight against England during the American Revolution. During the War Between the States, the Baptists were like many other Protestant denominations and split over the issue of slavery. This led to the birth of the Southern Baptist Convention and the Northern Baptist Convention (now the American Baptist Churches in the U.S.A.). The Baptist movement in the North had a strong appeal to the black community. As a result, it is now estimated that seven-eighths of the black population in the U.S. claim denominational affiliation to either the Baptist or Methodist church. In the US today, the four largest Baptist denominations are: The Southern Baptist Convention (15.4 million); the American Baptist Churches in the U.S.A. (1.5 million); and two African American denominations: the National Baptist Convention, U.S.A. Inc. (8.2 million); and the National Baptist Convention of America (3.5 million) (Brackney 1999). One of the controversial issues surrounding the Baptist movement is a select group of that denomination that laid claim to exclusive inspiration. They even went as far as claiming they were to be the "only" ones in heaven. This extremist claim gave them the nickname "Baptist Briders". They were given this name because they held to the belief that only those who were part of the Baptist church were to become the Bride of Christ mentioned in the book of Revelations. Several other religious denominations over the centuries have, as well, promoted that exclusive claim to heaven and the fallacy of exclusive inspiration. The Baptist denomination, however, does not hold these doctrines as part of their creed. Another issue that brought strains between Baptist believers was the acceptance or rejection of predestination and free will. As a result, separation in the movement took place during the 1800's. Still today the Free Will Baptists hold to their belief in free will (Baxter, 1957).

The "Old" Regular Baptist denomination was an independent division of Baptists who chose a more conservative path of faith and practice. It is a popular movement in Appalachia for it embraces "the old ways". The faith and practice of the Old Regular Baptist Church brings the flavor of Appalachian culture to the forefront.

"I would challenge every social worker that desires to work with the Appalachian culture to visit an Old Regular Baptist Service."

The largest movement of this denomination is in this author's home state of Kentucky, but has its roots in the Carolinas dating back to the 18th century. Understanding this denomination will give any social worker a good insight into the mountain culture. One of the staples of the mountains and most churches you will visit is music. The written music of the Old Regular Baptist church historically has no notes, lines or clefts. Each special song was handed down from member to member by tradition. Often hand-written words to songs were the only record of their existence. My first experience in an Old Regular Baptist church was a wonderful exposure to the Appalachian ways of worship. As we began the service, there were two singers who would sing a line of a song and the congregation would echo in return. The dissonance and minor chords of the music revealed a strong Celtic influence as does much of the music in Appalachia. Many of their songs are reminiscent of the Celtic folk songs familiar today (Dorgan, 1990).

The preaching style of the Regular Baptist is very distinctive with its singsong pattern of presentation that the people follow with great attention and excitement. There is usually little preparation of a sermon. The preachers rely on a "filling" to lead the direction of their sermon. Most preachers feel free to change the direction of a sermon in mid-stream. One of the unique practices I experienced was a good hand shaking from the minister while preaching. It is not uncommon for a preacher to make his way around the church while delivering his message. This tradition is a form of intimacy with each other in the church family.

"The worship experience of the mountain people took place only once every month. This time together was often their sole social experience for several weeks at a time."

A sermon may be 5 minutes or 2 hours. There were no expectations or time limits placed on the circuit-riding preachers who would travel from hollow to hollow and church to church. Quite unique in practice was the freedom of the congregation, lead by the Spirit, to begin a song at any time during the sermon. This practice called "singing down" a preacher was a small way of exercising their leadership of the Spirit in worship. It wasn't unusual for there to be several preachers who took the pulpit to preach on a given worship day. They would take turns preaching until the Spirit led them to conclude. Time was not an issue for the people. Because of their isolation in the mountains, they longed for the worship and fellowship. The distinct lack of formality and ceremony in worship speaks of the simple approach to both life and religion in Appalachia.

The Brethren faith

The Brethren or Moravians (people of German decent) were an industrious people. They were a tight, social family group who guarded their piety closely. Their denominational history precedes the rise of the Lutheran Reformation. After the Thirty-Years War, the people were finally free to explore religion and freedom of worship. Many Germans chose Catholicism, others Lutheranism and still others joined in with German Reformed traditions. Alexander Mack is a figure in the history of the Brethren who is given credit for initiating the "Movement". These groups of Brethren were called the "German Baptists" throughout the nineteenth century, and followed many of the Anabaptist traditions. They were also influenced by the piety of the Mennonite faith. One of their greatest stands was to have no creed other than what was taught in the New Testament.

There are three strong leaders spoken of in Brethren history. Around 1719, a man named Peter Becker brought a group of Brethren to America and planted their roots in Germantown, Pennsylvania. Alexander Mack came to the colonies later to lead the Germantown Brethren. History also speaks of another strong leader of the Brethren named John Naas who influenced the American Brethren in a new land. The Brethren in America set themselves apart from society as a whole. They were a very exclusive society. Being set apart meant abstaining from involvement in politics, "fancy dress", emblems or icons (religious ornaments in their church, jewelry or elsewhere), and musical instruments in their worship services. In regard to religious practice, they immersed their converts not just once, but three times. This practice gave them the nickname "Dunkers" by many of the main streams of society. So separated were they socially, that they were expected to marry only those of the Brethren faith. At the onset of the church, church discipline was very important to their society. The most minor punishment for those who "wandered" was called "stigmatization". A person being disciplined was allowed to attend worship, but they could not participate or fellowship with others in the congregation. A second practice was that of "disowning" a member. As a form of discipline, a person lost their membership in the church, but could come back to the flock if they chose to repent and change their lifestyle. A third and final form of discipline within the community of Brethren was a "shunning". This extreme tradition of totally disowning an individual meant both social and spiritual isolation (Bowman, 1995).

The Brethren made their life one of rural living in agricultural areas of the frontier. This being true, they had very little contact with the outside world. The growth of the Brethren spread to rural areas of Pennsylvania, Maryland, Virginia, North and South Carolina, Kentucky and Ohio. They enjoyed their solitude from society. One could very well make the comparison to the present day Appalachian people and the desire to live a secluded lifestyle. As the years progressed, so did the Brethren into a more liberalized denomination. Change did not come without controversy. Around 1881, the Old German Baptist Brethren parted in order to hold on to their pure and traditional teachings. Just two years later, the progressive members of the denomination formed the Brethren Church. This group was more concerned with education and evangelism. The more conservative branch of the Brethren also became more and more progressive. As the 1900's rounded the corner, the more conservative Dunkard Brethren united as a separate group in 1926 and the Fellowship of Grace Brethren Churches came together in 1939.

> *"Brethren groups continued to influence Appalachia, but very few of their congregations still dot our rural hills. Their tradition was that of building strong working communities. That hard working tradition is still an influence upon our culture."*

The Methodist movement

Methodism was a religious movement led by Charles Wesley, John Wesley and George Whitefield. Their inspiration to lead a new movement was derived from the apathy they saw within the Anglican Church. At Oxford University, the Wesley brothers and Whitefield had formed what they called the "Holy Club". Later, the beliefs of this religious society of young men were given the name Methodism. These young college theologians were pious young men sincere in their beliefs. Over the years, a variety of evangelical religious groups began to follow the theological views of the Wesley brothers and Whitefield. In opposition, several of the more conservative members of the Church of England in the mid-eighteenth century labeled their Methodist viewpoint heresy, opposing their view that an individual could be inspired and receive a personal revelation from God (Gill, 1964).

John Wesley was the most prominent of the three icons in the Methodist movement. He was the first of the "circuit rider" preachers. Stories are told of him traveling on horseback over thousands of miles, and preaching over forty thousand sermons. Most of his sermons were preached in open-air settings across the countryside. In his travels, he built up a large following. Most of those who followed him were from the laboring poor in the fast growing industrial areas of England. These people were the working class, which the Church of England had tended to neglect. By the late eighteenth century, there were hundreds of small chapels dotting the hillsides teaching Wesley's viewpoints.

> *"Methodism was very much a movement of the poor. The working class that had long been ostracized, now found solace within the church."*

Part of the growth of Methodism can be attributed to the many protests going on against the English Church. The other part can be attributed to the influence of the "Enlightenment". Religion was changing all across the face of England just like it was in America. The social and political issues that were important to the Methodists were few but powerful. Wesley had a very authoritarian outlook on raising children. Some Wesleyan followers supported child labor, yet other Methodists were more openly democratic and concerned with working class issues. They took an active role in politics and the development of trade unions. The movement stayed within the bounds of the Church of England until after John Wesley's death in 1791. It wasn't until 1932 that the United Methodist Church of Great Britain was established (Yrigoyen, 1996).

As with other denominations, their moral and ethical values influenced much of the English population. These values were soon to make their way to America. The movement had a great number of followers by the time politics in England began to stir, and therefore had much influence over the masses. One thing changed over the years. The denomination was no longer just that of the working poor. As the 19th century came, most of the movement consisted of artisans and craftsman. Other new converts were people in middle class occupations such as manufacturers and merchants. The movement continued to grow and include those of the upper class active in shaping English culture (McEllhenny, 1992).

"Every religious denomination somehow affects the political view of people. Whether directly or indirectly, we form our opinions based upon our moral standards."

The social and moral stands made by Wesley focused on bringing attention to the moral decay he saw within the country. He and his followers were determined to reform the morals of a nation. Their intervention for change was through evangelism and discipleship. It is not unusual for one man to affect change and bring influence to an entire culture. In this case, it was John Wesley who was the tool. Although he was an Oxford graduate who stayed active in the arts and humanities, his desire was to reach across education and economic lines to minister to the poor and unlearned. He believed that all men could have a personal experience with God.

John Locke was a secular philosopher who believed that personal experience was the source of knowledge. He stressed that a personal revelation of the truth or a personal experience of knowledge was the ultimate goal of man. There are many similarities between Locke's philosophy and Wesley's theology. It would not be far fetched to believe Locke's theory of personal knowledge, sense perception, and reasoning had some influence on Wesley and the Methodism movement. Many social workers regard Locke as an important philosopher from which many social theories are formed. The idea of self-determination is a core of what I call the Personal Experience Model. The Personal Experience Model is an approach to social work that will be explained in a second Book on social work practice in rural Appalachia (Young, 1998).

"I do state here though, that personal experience shapes both our social and religious outlook on life. For those of faith it is an emphasis on spiritual experience. For those who take a secular world-view, it is an emphasis on social interaction. Personal Experience influences every area of our life."

As we look at early America, we see Methodism strong and thriving in the 18th century. The "Great Awakening" was a surge of revivals that raised the Methodist church to prominence in Appalachia. The revival stressed the work of the Holy Spirit on human emotions and intellectual ideas. In 1801, history records a 2nd "Great Awakening" in Kentucky which saw the Presbyterian and Calvinistic Baptists convert over to the beliefs of the Methodist movement. Mountain people began to attend in great numbers at the Methodist and Freewill Baptist churches in the mid 1800's. Small churches began to spring up in rural hollows or mountain tops where people would came to worship God together (Bushman, 1989).

The Restoration Movement

The Stone-Campbell Restoration Movement is a religious reform movement that was born in the early 1800's. The name of the movement is taken from Barton W. Stone and Alexander Campbell. These two men of faith are considered the leading figures of several independent movements. They held to very similar principles which brought them closer together into two religious movements of significant size. One of the strongest principles of the Restoration Movement was that Christianity should not be divided. Their ultimate goal was to see the church as a whole and serving God with one heart and mind. That is still their focus today. They do not call themselves a denomination, for they believe creeds that denominationalism promotes also divide the body of Christ. Their simple message is that Christians should be able to agree on the basic principles of the Bible itself instead of on opinions and interpretations of the Bible (Foster, Blowers, Dunnavant, and Williams 2004).

Another strong belief is that traditions of the church also divide. Believers should be able to find common ground by following the practices of the early church. Further, the names that we place on our churches are often of man's design and produce schisms and division within the church. Unity is found when Christians find common grounds in the faith instead of differences.

"Churches, like any other social entity, are made of people whose human nature is bent on having differing interpretations of practice and polity."

The Christian Churches of the 1800's lead by Elias Smith and Abner Jones were contemporaries of a minister named James O'Kelly. They found that their commonalities were stronger than their differences and so history calls their coming together the "Christian Connection". In 1826, they joined with others in the Restoration Movement. The strongest of leaders in this movement were Barton Stone and Alexander Campbell. It seems that the Christian Connection and Alexander Campbell had a falling out several years after coming together. Some members of the Christian Connection stayed with Campbell and Stone and others joined themselves with the Congregational Churches. In the 1950's, they merged with other congregations to become the United Church of Christ. As the movement grew, there were many issues that brought about division between the Church of Christ and the Disciples of Christ. One of the issues of disagreement was the belief in exclusivism. A second issue arose in the movement when there was a special called meeting of a group of churches in Cincinnati, Ohio. They met there to form a general church organization. This added fuel to the fire of division for "organizations" had long been dissolved among the churches (Mead and Hill 2001).

Midway, Kentucky was the site of a Church of Christ where a piano was brought into the service for worship. Until this time, worship was done without music. This began the dispute over whether instruments should or should not be used in worship. The seeds were planted for the recognition of Non-Instrumental Churches of Christ. There are many Church of Christ Non-Instrumental in the Appalachian area.

The Church of Christ Non-Institutional is a name given to those who objected to the oversight of the church's individual activities by any other church or institution. Specifically, they disagreed with the pooling of money into any fund or account that would be overseen by one church but supported by a group of churches. It was their belief that an independent church should not join into any venture that would lead it to be considered an institution.

The final group that will be mentioned here is the Crossroads Movement, which began in Gainesville, Florida in the 1960's and 1970's. It began as a radical, yet widely accepted, movement within the church. One of the main focuses of the movement was prayer, prayer cells, a focus on revitalizing smaller churches and outreach ministries to Universities and Colleges. History tells of a Boston area church that began outreach and church planting ministries in large cities using the same principles of the Crossroads Movement. These Pillar Churches began to plant their roots and expand into what became known as the Boston Movement. The mainstream Church of Christ denounced the Boston Movement because they added discipleship as a mandatory process prior to Baptism. Secondly, it was the desire of the movement to go International with the appointment of World Sector leaders to oversee the Church of Christ's interest internationally (Foster, Blowers, Dunnavant and Williams 2004).

> *"Through the years, the members of the Church of Christ still hold strong to their belief of unity over diversity. Today the Church of Christ is strong and for the most part are strong independent and autonomous churches."*

How do we bring it all together?

Other churches, not mentioned in detail, grew strong at the turn of the 20th century. Historical mission efforts were common in Appalachia where mainstream denominations saw a need for the "mountain people" to be reached. Their home mission boards looked at the small autonomous churches as those who needed the help of a more prosperous and educated organization. In the early 1900's, denominations began to send their missionaries into the mountains to help reach the people. Thus, missionary churches of every denomination sprang up throughout rural areas of the Appalachian Mountains and their foothills. This chapter has been quite lengthy in regard to the history of a few religious influences in Appalachia, but to know the norms, values and beliefs of religion in the region allows the social work professional to understand the roots of its people.

> *"To know the major religious influences that drive a culture is to know from what rose colored glasses they view life."*

There are not enough pages or libraries to contain the endless church histories that could be written. This is not just a chapter on church history. What it is, however, is a piece of the puzzle for social practice. Appalachia is a culture shaped by their belief. The culture in Appalachia is rich with faith and a religious zeal that is the influence of generation after generation of mountain family. The bottom line is this:

> *"Appalachia is a culture shaped by religious beliefs. You cannot study the social life of Appalachian people without studying the history of their faith. Study it well, for it will give you a peek into their soul."*

CHAPTER FIVE

RELIGION AND SOCIAL DILEMMA:
Extreme beliefs that create social quandary

Appalachia is truly a culture shaped by its beliefs. Those beliefs can be a powerful force for good, yet an influence for personal struggle when misguided. If you have approached this text from a secular worldview, I invite you to <u>not</u> look at it skeptically. The thoughts contained herein will be of value in understanding those in your care who are strong in their faith. If you are approaching this text as a person of faith, it may seem to be a critique of denominations and doctrinal beliefs or a slam at apologetics. It is not. **The views shared in this chapter are, however, a look at some of the <u>distorted views</u> that arise when these beliefs are embraced <u>to the extreme</u> and those that generate social problems and quandary in their wake.**

"What God means for goodness of fit in the life of his children, man often bends into a burden."

I must clearly state that this chapter is based upon observations made after years of counseling and social work in both a religious and secular world. Many of these thoughts are from the viewpoint of those who may not approach the social sciences from a Judeo-Christian perspective. These are the consequences and outcomes seen in the lives of those with whom I have worked over the years. These views are a merge of both secular and religious worldviews. One would think that the only thing spawned from our faith and practice is positive. From experience, I must say that this is not always true. Some of the first social dilemmas to which I will speak are negative self-concepts and fatalistic outlooks on life.

"Organized religion has and probably always will elicit some negative affect upon the lives of those who embrace their religious beliefs to the extreme and create a quandary with their faith."

When I speak of the extreme, I speak of those who would make us strain at a gnat and swallow a camel. I would like it to be as clear as possible when I say: There is a major difference between "religion" and "faith". You can quote this: "There are people who are so heavenly minded they are of no earthly good." What does that mean? There are people who spend all their time living in a religious world, where their own personal and eternal value is based upon a list of what they "do" and "don't do". The most important thing in life to them is to live a separated pious life. They spend so much time doing things in the name of heaven, that they neglect the most important things on earth. They neglect their earthly responsibilities believing their sacrifice will somehow bring them closer to God and heaven. All such neglect does is create social problems within our home and social environment. God created the family before he created the church, and He expects us to be mindful of our earthly responsibilities.

> "Social problems do not fix themselves simply because we embrace religion. We can't allow ourselves to believe such extreme ideals as: 'once we embrace faith our problems disappear', but faith does provide an avenue toward social and spiritual goodness of fit."

You can find at least one "extremist", authoritarian or legalistic church leader within any given denomination. Who we pay less attention to are those people influenced negatively by these extreme, authoritarian and legalistic leaders. In every culture and generation, people have been taught extreme "religious" views which they must adhere to for eternal peace and must embrace them as infallible truth. When you hear something long enough you begin to believe it! To their detriment, many followers have been burdened with unrealistic expectations that create social quandary and dilemma in their life. The Apostle Paul of Bible fame wrote many times about the unrealistic expectations "church leaders" were placing on the people. His words were "why do you try to test God by putting on the necks of the people a yoke that neither we or God intended for them to wear?" (Galatians 4:10). In the next chapter, he talks to a group of Christians who chose to follow the "rules" of men rather than the freedom found in true faith. He stated that it was like trading freedom for slavery.

The observations in this chapter should not be taken as an affront to denominational beliefs, as writings on apologetics, or as a slam on church doctrine. These observations are simply that: observations. As social workers, we need to learn to see the social connections between faith, religion and social interaction. I challenge you to read with an open mind and heart.

> "The religious and secular worldviews we embrace are based often on our interpretations of environment and experience. Those interpretations are often not our own, but those we accept from people of influence in our lives. Many choose a secular worldview because a religious society has turned them off by their extreme approach to life and living."

As we interpret and incorporate spiritual ideals into our life, we choose lifestyles that create a goodness of fit or lack of fit! As we listen to others who interpret it and pass it on to us, we choose to accept it, reject it, apply it or modify it. Regardless of your own views, I ask you to examine the following social quandaries and dilemmas created by spiritual beliefs and value systems as they are taken to an extreme with many of the people of rural Appalachia. Whether you agree or disagree with statements made in this chapter, please take the time to think them through before discarding them. Stay strong to your own value system, but see if what's said sheds light on the attitudes you find within the Appalachian culture. Whether you accept or reject these thoughts, you have been exposed to a new theory on social dilemmas.

Predetermined Favor or Fatalism?

How does fatalism result from a religious teaching? Just the thought that God would pre-determine the ones who will accept him and the ones who will reject him may cause us to begin asking questions: "Am I one of those who will be rejected by God or accepted by God? Am I standing in the balances and found wanting? Am I a person who is worthy enough to be selected for heaven?" Regardless of my faith and practice or whether you are a person of faith at all, the dilemma for people who are troubled by these thoughts is the promotion of a fatalistic viewpoint on life. What is the thinking? In counseling, I have had some state: "If only a few of us are predestined to make it to heaven, then what is the use in trying?" I have strong beliefs on this issue, but I also must acknowledge a social dilemma for those whose worldviews are steeped with emotions of hopelessness. The tragedy and truth is that many buy into the lie that their life and future is hopeless. When they buy into this apathetic outlook on life, they give up on attempts to better themselves. They embrace attitudes and life styles of careless living and thus create social quandary in their life. How then do social workers address such a dilemma in light of our approach to people of faith? We address it through empowerment and self-determination.

"A social worker must find people where they are and help them find their way to where they should be. We deal daily with those who have chosen careless life styles, and often those choices were made because of their fatalistic view of life."

When we find people in need of change, our role as change agent arises. I really do not believe that our people are being "led astray" like the pied piper by some fatalistic doctrine. I do believe that the view of "why try" has been past on from generation to generation. I do believe, out of naivety, some believe their future and life are hopeless. I have counseled with adults and teens that say: "I can't do any better". It was not uncommon for me in practice to have visited some of my fathers with no education and hear them say: "Why should I get an education, there are no jobs here anyway?" Many of my mothers have said: "I know I only have 60 months of support under the new welfare plan, but I will worry about that when the time comes." There are wives who are living in co-dependant relationships where physical abuse is accepted as their lot in life. The only outcome for those who embrace this fatalistic view of life is a life of harmful consequence. Whether spurred by religious teaching, learned helplessness or negativism from birth, fatalism is strong in Appalachia.

When a person lives with being knocked down time after time, they begin to believe that what they are handed in life cannot be changed. Life seems to be "fatal" therefore why try! Day after day they go on believing the best things in life are for someone else. Giving your best does not always put you on top of the world. Giving your best does not always produce the recognition and reward deserved. The hardest thing for a social worker is to have to admit it to be true. I tell my own children that "whoever told you life is fair told you a lie". That is where the social worker steps up to help empower those who need them.

"One of the most important focuses for practice in social work is helping those in our care rise out of the social dilemmas holding them down. We can not remove the consequences of careless living, but we can empower them with the tools to work through them!"

Our goal is to help promote self-realization and self-determination. We must help <u>them</u> identify their issues, make change and help them rise above their fatalistic viewpoint of life. If we can give them hope and help them cope, perhaps those interventions will challenge them to buy into the dream of making a difference with their life. We gladly embrace the role of change agent because we believe people can make a change. One of my hardest leaps from ministry to social work was not imposing my Judeo-Christian ethics upon others. Legislating morality to those with whom we work is always tempting for a social worker who has strong spiritual beliefs. But I also strongly believe our goal in social work practice is to help move a hurting world toward self-determination not always conversion. This is sort of an outside in approach, but a self-determined soul will see truth in our altruistic approach of outreach.

It could best be explained by a conversation I had with a friend when I chose the path of social work as a career instead of full-time ministry. The friend asked: "Why did you leave the ministry?" My reply was, "I didn't." A social workers worldview approaches practice with ideals of feeding the hungry, clothing the naked, visiting the widow, caring for the orphans and so much more. The only thing people of faith in social work do differently is serve from a site without a steeple. If we can change the fatalistic view of a person in quandary, then we have done social work. **If we understand an individual's worldview, we can better implement change and potential success in case management. When we understand their faith, we have discovered another tool to bring them hope.**

Perfectly Sinless?

One of the most shocking statements I've heard in working with people here in Appalachia came from a "religious" man who stated: "Since I found religion I've not sinned once." As absurd as this may sound, it is a view held by many.

"The view of sinless perfection is taken from some who believe that when you become a person of faith, God transforms you into a 'sinless being'."

A pretty serious social quandary arises from this "superiority complex" interpretation, or "inferiority fallacy" if you will. Although not a popular viewpoint, it too promotes a fatalistic view on life. There are those who believe they can live a sinless life once they have had a religious experience. There are also those on the flip side who believe a Holy God will never accept them. Living with this former attitude means living in defeat all your life.

While working on my graduate degree, I took my first good look at the DSM IV. One of the diagnoses that intrigued me was the Narcissistic condition. This condition causes a person to be "drunk" with power and perfection. How many times during your life have you run across those whose word was law and whose will was not to be questioned? I have seen it many times within realms of social work, education and the church. Preaching in my childhood hometown was a man whose charisma launched him into the place of "god" to his people. They followed him to isolation and death. Jim Jones was that type of narcissistic leader. These types of people are leaders who choose to defy society and sanity for the sake of their spiritual ego, and people follow them without question. We only need to look at similar cult activity in the last decade to see its extreme consequences. This condition reflects the far extreme of which I speak. On one extreme are those who have the audacity to claim infallibility of word and deed, and on the other side are those who follow "under foot". In regard to their superior perceptions, they teach it, preach it, and practice it. In regard to the inferiority fallacy, there will always be those who follow it, break under it and live in defeat. Our generation has seen the rise and fall of these kinds of leaders both political and religious. They think they are above the law and the Lord when they take their "own will" and impress it upon others. It happens from the home to the pulpit and those who say they speak for God impose their superior perspective of guidance to the world around them.

"Living in defeat is a social dilemma for those who are easily influenced and led in the name of spiritual guidance by those who see themselves as perfectly without fault or sin."

How do you know the difference? The answer lies in identifying those who lift themselves up to keep others down. The idea that one particular person is always right necessitates that everyone else is wrong, putting them at the bottom of societies chain. On the flip side, a person who can do no wrong in their own eyes has placed himself or herself above reality. And you say this is a result of religious influence? Yes. Great men like Luther, Huss, Wesley and others mentioned in this book realized they fell short. Their goodness of fit was found in the belief that there was an eternal being that would catch them before they hit the bottom. The history of religion in Appalachia found in this book is not all about history. It is an insight into what made the Appalachian mountain family strong. Fighting the defeatist attitude on life is one of the strongest character qualities used to keep the mountain people mighty in the face of weakness.

Those who buy into the "I'll never hit the mark" idea are being cheated in life. They live with the fatalistic view that no matter how hard you work you will always fall short. We are all born with an innate knowledge that we can never be perfect. Therefore, the teaching that some can be and some cannot be perfect automatically places some in the heavenlies and some "under foot". The Apostle Paul wrote: "we all fall short of the glory of God" (Romans 3:23). Being intrigued by athletics and the Roman games of the time, Paul used this archery term, which meant we could never hit the bulls-eye of perfection. Outside of our own personal relationship with a loving God we ALL fall short! He was right, and here is the dilemma. The person living with a fatal view of life settles for less than the best. They believe they will never amount to anything. They feel alone and go through life with no desire to try changing their life style or social status. There is no need to better self, because they believe success can never be achieved. There is no need to obtain and EPO (Emergency Protective Order) against an abusive spouse because "this is what life has handed me". "There is no need to bring a social worker into our home to expose the family secret of sexual abuse. This is my lot in life so why report it." I have faced this type of individual more than I really want to in my years of counseling and social work. One of the hardest people to empower is the one who does not think they are worth it. All their lives they have been taught God loves them out of pity because they are not perfect.

God has blessed me with two beautiful daughters. In my mind they were God's perfect gift, yet I knew they would never be able to live a perfect life. From the time they were born, daddy treated them like a "princess", and I prayed intently that they would not get caught up in the world's idea of what beauty and perfection is for women. Yet, through the years we have and will always fight the self-concept battle against the world's ideal. Hopefully reality will win over the perfection fallacy. I challenge us all to understand that there are none perfect, NOT A ONE!

The role of the change agent is to reach out to those who feel less perfect. Unless you have been living in a "locked box", our goal as social workers is to bring power to the powerless. We must bring hope to the hopeless. As social workers, we must offer peace to those in turmoil. We must show them that none of us can live a life that is perfect. We do make choices in life and some of those choices bring good consequences and some of them produce bad consequences. When the bad times come, it is not because we are of less value than others!

"Whether the idea of being 'less than perfect' is past on from generation to generation or by religious views gone bad, WE MUST KNOW THAT LIFE IS FULL AND WE ARE PERFECTLY LOVED."

Our role as change agent and broker is to understand the role religion plays in a person's worldview. If we understand their worldview, we can understand better how to develop intervention strategies for goodness of fit.

The Priesthood of the believer?

What in the world does this term mean? It is the idea that any believer can interpret the Bible for him or herself. All believers can come before God without the assistance of a Preacher, Priest or Pope. The common man or woman can determine for themselves the direction of their spiritual life without it being legislated or imposed. Basically, the believer needs no one but him or herself to carry on a relationship with the creator. That is what the Priesthood of the believer is all about. I have counseled a whole generation of people who march to the beat of someone else's drum. They believe what they believe based on what they are told to believe rather than choosing to think on their own.

How is this social quandary? They register as a Democrat, Republican or third party because of someone else's influence. They have strong denominational ties not because of doctrinal conviction, but because they have been told what to believe. "Well the preacher said we ought to ____". You finish the phrase. People look up to those who they see as spiritual leaders and mimic their ideals without ever stopping to examine what they believe for themselves. You only have to look at the type of cult activities already mentioned along with others like David Koresh at Waco Texas and the Halley's Comet Cult to see that people are likely to believe and follow any idea. Though quite extreme, these leaders persuaded people who were searching for answers. They just had the wrong answers. We must be very careful that we do not allow others to be prophet, priest and king of our life.

"In social work, we teach self-sufficiency, independence for the co-dependant and self-determination for those whose ability to choose has been squashed. We rally behind the term 'empowerment' without really knowing the freedom that comes when our clients live empowered lives."

We are all influenced by the thoughts and teachings of others. This doesn't mean that our belief system is necessarily wrong. What I am saying is that: "Every man must be fully persuaded in his own heart." (Romans 14:5) Where scripture is silent, we have to be silent. If the scripture doesn't speak it, neither should we. And truly no man can claim to be the "divine" voice of God on matters that are not already clear in scripture. A person who claims they have some "new insight" from God might as well try to take the place of God.

"The social worker who doles out advice as infallible is on dangerous ground. They have no right to put a bit in the mouths of others to guide them where they do not want to go."

What is the plight of the victims who adopt blind obedience to those who would seek to control them? Their quandary is a seemingly endless lifestyle of submission and co-dependency. They choose to live a continuous cycle of trying to follow the legalistic "rules" of men. There are many innocent people who are led astray and do not have the cognitive or social skills to know the difference between sincerely good direction and legalistic manipulation. The idea that one man or one denomination has a corner on legislating lifestyles, interpreting scripture, controlling the will of a person, dominating the direction of a church or an entire social circle is careless. To say that one man or one organization has a corner on how each of us must live our life is also careless.

If we are to reach out to those who are easily manipulated, we must understand their spirit and who or what influences and controls them. If our clients have any Judeo-Christian worldview whatsoever, we must teach them the difference between religion and faith. We must teach them to be freethinking individuals. One of the things that awakened my desire to search the scripture, as a young man was this: I did not know why I believed what I believed. My years of Bible study and degrees in Theology are of no value to me if I am to be told my own interpretation of scripture doesn't count. This is the driving thought that spurred Martin Luther to take a stand. He believed that everyone has the right to read and interpret for him or herself. How does this relate to a social dilemma? It has to do with self-determination. As a therapist, I cannot tell someone what to do! I cannot tell them that my interventions are law, because my diagnosis is not infallible. People must choose to make a change in their life, not change because someone else has it in their best interest. They need to be taught to draw their own conclusion about their life situations.

"Self-determination must take place before they can step onto the road of recovery and goodness of fit. This principle is so valued that it was placed in the creed of the National Association of Social Work."

The value of each individual is so universal that Abraham Lincoln included it in the Gettysburg Address when he said, "all men are created equal". He meant that there is no division of importance with social class. Sometimes people of faith unintentionally create another social class and draw a line between themselves and those "yet to believe". Although their motivation may be sincere, it often becomes legalistic. The goal is to say "let me show you a faith that will love you just the way you are". The legalistic insinuation heard is: "If you want to be part of this church, you must listen to Gods man and follow the church covenant". When a person of faith claims they are on a mission to reach out to others there is a barometer by which you can measure sincerity. I see two obvious and simple outcomes. Is their effort to reach out in the name of God or is it to "make them like us" or "convince them to believe like me"? Which is right? **My suggestion is to keep your eyes off man and keep them focused above. As a social worker, we have to focus on the influences and life experiences of those with whom we work.**

"To know the influences under which our clients live, and to understand what is shaping their self-concept gives us an edge on how to intervene."

Eternal happiness based upon works?

There are many questions that run through our minds when we think about end of life issues. Is there life after death? Does heaven really exist? Have I earned eternal happiness? The inevitable statement has been made throughout human history: "I hope I've done enough good things to make it to heaven". Regardless of your religious belief, an eternal destiny based upon good works has been part of religious dogma for centuries. If we believe works bring us happiness and heaven, then we have created a social dilemma for ourselves. We are saying our value in life and the hereafter is based upon what I do or don't do, not who I am.

There are many altruistic people in our world, and they make a difference in life because of their generosity. But they are not buying their way to heaven. Being a humanitarian is not just giving, it is having a spirit of helping. In her long years of ministry, Mother Teresa spent almost all of her time with the widows, poor, and helpless. Should we be any different than she? What an example! I believe we have a duty to help the helpless, clothe the cold and needy and seek housing for the homeless. It is not, however, our ticket to heaven. Doing good deeds does not make us of great value to society. Our value to society lies in the spirit of giving not the deed. What is the social quandary regarding this issue? The thought that our self-worth is based on self-works makes a person feel like they have to earn their way to happiness. Wouldn't that simply promote the idea that we can pay our way to heaven by good works? Our works without true faith is dead!

Every year when people visited the angel tree in our Family Resource Center to adopt children at Christmas time, our joy was to be able to deliver those special gifts and see the bitter sweetness of thanks and yet regret upon the faces of parents who could not provide for their children. Yes, real men do cry. I couldn't help but weep when I saw in their eyes the sincere hope that they will someday be able to "give back". The real truth is that they probably will never be able to give. When a person's socioeconomic status does not allow them to be a "giver", a sense of hopelessness and unworthiness are the outcomes. Many of the families with whom I worked day in an out, live with the belief that they are of no worth because they have nothing to give back to society. They live in poverty with nothing above a crumb to give away. They have a hard time hiding their feelings of inadequacy and unworthiness, but they do hide. They hide from society. They are ashamed to reach out, so they live with unacceptable circumstances. Pride often gets in the way and people often refuse to accept the much-needed help they deserve. I have had some say: "I feel bad because I am taking from others all the time. I don't have anything to give back!"

"Whether intentional or not, society does place a higher social value on those with wealth. Those who 'have' are served, and those who 'have not' do the serving. You don't have to look very far in our society to acknowledge that what I say is true."

It is good to hear an offering prayer that says "God bless those who give and those who can not". If we believe worth to society is based on material giving, our families have no chance to be of value. Because they live with a defeated attitude, their outlook on life is apathetic. There is no earthly happiness for them. So, why would there be eternal happiness? By knowing their worldview and the reality of their life situation, we can become the change agent they need. They <u>are</u> the poor, the helpless, and the homeless. If the truth be known and given a choice, they would rather be givers than takers. Sadly, they have nothing to give. Our role as change agent is to help them know that they ALL are of worth and value. They must know that they can contribute to society if they choose. We need to help them redefine value and worth as intrinsic.

"Success and worth in this world are not measured by what we accumulate here. Success and worth are based upon how we invest in the lives of others."

Investment is what makes a true social worker. Success is not about what we accumulate at the end of our life. Success is based on what we did on the journey! We cannot choose social work as a means of meeting our own intrinsic need to be needed. That motivation is selfish. **We must empower our clients with the message of worth, value and determination to better themselves. Their human worth is not based on works.**

Is it free will, free license or responsible living?

The free will of man has been a topic of religious discussions for centuries. In it's truest sense, it teaches that within each of us we have the will to make choices in life. In social work terms it is the belief in self-determination. If we were to choose synonyms for the word self-determination, it would probably be freewill, autonomy, self-government, independence or freedom. On the surface, it is the commonly held belief that all men and women have the free will to decide for themselves the truth on life issues. How then can this be a social dilemma? Follow this train of thought if you can. One of my clients stated: "If God has given me a free will to choose my course in life, then no one has the right to tell me what is right and wrong." For those who take free will to this extreme, their will becomes their license to live as they choose.

How many times have you heard a strong willed child say: "You're not my boss!" They then proceed to make a bad choice in behavior. Some people have no care of how their freewill choices affect others. It is a selfish point of view that sees the only goal in life as fulfilling what feels good and meets their needs. We are all born with "...certain inalienable rights". Our rights do not include the right to do what our will chooses. We do not have the right or freedom to yell, "Fire!" in a crowded building. We cannot live a lifestyle that bends or breaks the will of others. We do not have the freedom to impose our will on other people. But that strong will to dominate is the "good-ole-boy" philosophy taught to many of our young Appalachian men. "I'm the man of the house...you'll do what you are told." Thus, a life of servitude and subjugation of women and children becomes acceptable.

The idea that women and children are to keep silent in the church is quite strong here in Appalachia. This is the attitude that I am faced with in rural Appalachia. "Don't you come in here and tell me what is right and wrong. If I want to lay the rod to my "youngins", I will! The Bible tells me to not spare the rod. That is my right as a father, and I'll break that child's will if it's the last thing I do." Free will is not a license to do what we want in life and society. Jude, an author of scripture, stated: "godless men have slipped in and have changed the grace of God into a license." (Jude 4) Paul of New Testament fame started a church in a town called Galatia and was faced with this very issue. He told them: "Do not use your freedom as an occasion to do what ever you choose". What is the lesson? The end does NOT justify the means just because it seems right to us. The free love movement of the 60's attempted to promote the idea that "if it feels good, do it". Regardless of the messages we may hear from free-willing theologians or from a free-willing society, we <u>are</u> right in equating free will with self-determination. As social workers, we want to encourage our clients to have a strong will and adopt a responsible lifestyle. What is it we want to empower them with? We want them to make wise choices with their lives, but we can't make them choose wisely.

I like to rewrite old quotes. One of my favorite re-writes of the quote: "Your can lead a horse to water, but you can't make it drink" is "You can lead a horse to water, and you can make it <u>desirable</u> to drink! **Where we go wrong in intervention is when we try to force people into compliance. Unless it has to do with the law, people do have a free will to choose what burdens they carry or what victories they claim.**

> *"Our job as change agent, broker and teacher is to identify when our clients are out there on the extreme edge and mark them. When we teach them responsible living, their choices will be positive. It's called empowerment."*

Does generalist practice and faith blend?

A simple answer would be yes. Both faith and social work practice look at the interconnected systems in the lives of individuals, families, social groups, communities and even from a global perspective which we might call the uttermost parts of the earth. Both generalist practice and faith take a holistic approach to promoting wisdom/knowledge, values, and skills to navigate the world in which we live and to tackle problems in life through a planned change process. Whether through a problem solving framework or through eyes of faith, there are MANY similarities between a faith based approach to life and our highly valued generalist practice model. Approaching social work in rural America from both a generalist practitioner viewpoint and a theological perspective, you see the best and the worse of both worlds. You will see "religion" not faith in church ministry as well as in social work practice. You will also experience true faith in action within the church and social work field. There is a difference!

> *"From a social perspective, blending both is like the difference between 'knowing' social theory and 'practicing' social work. One is the matter of knowledge and one is the matter of practice. So it is with understanding faith in practice in the life of your client. Knowing which is which in the life of your client is a valuable tool for both evaluation and intervention."*

This is what I have learned over the years. There is a major difference in the goodness of fit of individuals who have a social foundation and support system founded in their faith. **Religion shapes our life in Appalachia, and we shape our religion.** When an individual finds comfort in their faith, it makes a world of difference. Appalachian churches are like snowflakes with each church being unique and different. Since each individual is also different and unique, the crayon box of church types meets the social needs of many. People of faith will eventually find their spiritual and social niche. Culture and religion are one in the same here. It is hard to separate them.

"As a social worker identifies and understands the support systems found in faith, they will be able to use this system of faith as one of their strongest tools for social change."

So then what is the answer? Religion and generalist practice **do** mix. Often the answer to social dilemma comes back to religious influence. Society and Social reformers tend to see those who attack social problems with faith as weak. They often perceive religious influences as a hindrance to social progress. What reformers often do not understand is that faith, belief and religious value help the Appalachian people hold on to and sustain a meaningful existence within a life that often has no meaning. Challenging life experiences have made the Appalachian people a resilient culture. You would have to become a student of social dilemmas in Appalachia to know that the people need their faith to provide them a peace that passes all understanding. They need a faith that promises a future and one that will endure to future generations. The Hebrew nation was strong on tradition and those traditions (life practices) produced a goodness of fit for a nation. Likewise, the Appalachian people have handed down a way of life and traditions of faith that produce a goodness of fit.

This culture includes not just oral tradition but written tradition and faith founded in scripture. This book has touched the lives of generations. Believer after believer shared their conversion with others, and a world was opened to a message of hope. That message transcended cultures and nationalities. It continues to do the same today. Not only have the Appalachian people past on a traditional value system, but they also pass down a strong religious belief system. This passing down of the faith is the very foundation of Appalachia. Appalachia is Ablaze with a people shaped by their faith.

Where does generalist practice blend with religion? Generalist practice takes into account social, economic, racial, gender and religious influences and recognizes that, within a person's environment, the individual is influenced by the interaction and interdependence of others. For this study, it is the detailed interaction of religious influences that often defines the Appalachian people. A person's soul renewed by their faith is a real influence of one system upon another. A person's spiritual influence (the church) is an interdependent group of persons interacting upon each other. They are bound together by doctrine, faith and practice into a "system" which functions to bring goodness of fit to more than one person in the system. Understanding what this system holds as valuable helps us as social workers know how to counsel and offer support.

As mentioned before, the church often becomes a surrogate family. As with a family, each person in the church naturally takes on a role of his or her own. Each person fits into their place based upon their God given gift. Each autonomous church family has its own goal, mission and personality. Each person in that system takes on a role of leadership or service. Each church has its evolved set of rules under which it operates, often written in by-laws, constitutions or covenants. Yes, they even sometimes include forms of discipline. Understanding how a church family works and influences those in our care will give us wisdom on how to reach them. Church family is far more than just a group of individuals meeting together to pray.

"Within that mezzo system are micro systems of friendship and support. Put together, they are a macro system of denominations. Joined once more they are a macro body of believers. They are a system of influence upon each other."

Let's talk about systems boundaries. A study of Appalachian churches will give you a clear understanding of the general systems principle of systems boundaries. Most of the individual autonomous church families hold tight to imaginary open borders or imaginary walls around them. They allow people to enter in or exclude them from entering. People within the "system" decide who is accepted and who is not accepted into the "fellowship of the church". The beauty of a social worker understanding the workings of faith and practice is that it allows us to understand the goodness of fit it brings into the lives of others or the lack of fit when taken to the extreme. Within the church family, more so than a community, people find those boundaries open and inviting. People are welcome and find the support system all-inclusive. And yes, we often find the opposite. We often find a closed system unwilling to let others in or members out.

We have talked extensively about some of the social barriers and burdens imposed upon people within the "church system". Our society will probably never be rid of those types of church systems. They will always be controlling. Our people will often be exposed to a system that places burdens upon others that are too grievous to bear. The wonderful part of faith and practice, however, is the good always out weighs the bad. The faith of the Appalachian people holds us strong and empowered. This is what makes understanding the influences of the church so important to social work. Generalist practice and religion do mix. A person who approaches life from a secular worldview has found his or her own goodness of fit and social well being from another source. A person's goodness of fit, or lack of fit in life, is not always measured by their faith and what they believe or don't believe. The point I make here is simply goodness of fit or lack of fit for many is strongly influenced by how people relate to their religious ties. The bottom line is this:

> *"Spiritual belief, at it's root level, does not create social turmoil in the life of an individual. The truth is just the opposite. It is a change agent in itself! When we know the truth, the truth will set us free. There is great value in social work practice for understanding the spiritual mindset of those with whom we work. It gives us a powerful tool for professional practice."*

CHAPTER SIX

EXPRESSIONS OF THE APPALACHIAN CULTURE:
The roots of Appalachian music, art and craft

As we look at the many areas that affect change and development of culture, music is at the top of the list here in Appalachia. Appalachian music carries a concentration of both the traditionalism of "old-time" music and the newness of modern country. How does music relate to the social development of culture? Music is a powerful tool for the expression of social ideals, standards and even history. In the development of "mountain music", an entire nation was sold on the picture painted in the public eye. When I say "mountain music" what picture comes to mind? I would venture a bet that many readers pictured old men with fiddle in hand, corn cob pipes in their mouth with smoke ascending, adorned on head are pointed hats with feathers, on their bibbed overalls are quilt patches and at least one person is blowing into a moonshine jug. How right was I?

During the growth of mountain music in our nation, many of the radio and music halls pressured performers to play the part of the "hillbilly" when they performed. In fact, most of the performers who first made the music popular were not musicians from the rural hills at all, but professional musicians. Whether we like it or not, the "country bumpkin" stereotype took hold and became a good marketing tool for this type of music.

"Societies buy into the stereotyping of a people, and they do it willingly. We could site many other cultural stereotypes to make the point here, but the truth remains that it goes on in the public eye!"

Not all marketing of the musical culture was negative. There was a positive side as well. What was it that really influenced the music itself? The growing immigrant population was one of the first influences to our "mountain music". Country music's image as "An American Tradition" began to take shape as other nationalities began to buy into a new style of music. They helped to mold the style of music by adding their cultural individuality. Bluegrass music had its start in the rural south after World War II. Bluegrass was basically a fusion of "hillbilly", "folk", "Celtic" and various types of "country" that was embraced by rural families and working class people. Just as I call Appalachia the crayon box of culture, so was the musical heritage of the immigrants who influenced the music and art of our region from its conception.

Appalachian art is probably as unique as any art form in the world. As I became aware of my own Appalachian roots and moved to Eastern Kentucky, music and art of the region showed itself to me as a crayon box expression of personality. To use an analogy of my own, I describe it as this:

> *"Everyone is born with the God-given gift of individuality. When we begin to express that individuality in relation to our culture, environment, religion and the life influences from which we take value, it merges into personality!"*

The individuality of the Appalachian people is not as much individuality as it is personality. It is the merging together of LIFE! What comes out of that merge is unique and beautiful. We have already spoken of the expression of religion. A more visible expression of our Appalachian personality is what we find in music and art. This section is a look at a few of those enriching expressions.

What is old-time music?

There is no real clear-cut definition of old-time music, except that it is a type of rural music handed down in isolated areas of the Appalachian Mountains. The two main instruments used in old-time music were the banjo and fiddle. These main instruments that give individuality to Old-time music came from outside our nation. The banjo and its style of play came from Africa. The fiddle came from Western Europe, specifically, Germany, Scotland and Ireland. With their coming to America, the fiddle and banjo gained quick popularity in the mountains. Several stories come to light after reading the history of the Banjo. One version speaks of white traveling musicians who made the banjo popular as they traveled the mountains and urban areas before the Civil War. It gained further popularity with veterans coming home from the war. Version two is more believable. Knowing the origin of the banjo, I am inclined to believe that African American masters of the banjo taught white American musicians the art and style of play. If you are a student of music, you will find that there are many commonalities between earlier black banjo players and mountain banjo players who made the music popular. There were very few recordings made of the African-American bands that played the old-time string music. There are still a few commercial recordings in circulation where African-American and European-American musicians played together (Conway, 1995).

In the mountains, the fiddle came into popularity after the war. It is likely that some of the first "duets" played with fiddle and banjo also originated with African-Americans. Their love for the music was a diversion from the burden of slavery. As we saw the fiddle growing in popularity, we catch a taste of the influence of Celtic music. The fiddle was well loved and used almost solely in their musical expressions.

The guitar and mandolin were introduced into mountain music in the late 19th century. With the addition of other instruments such as accordions, pianos, dobros, dulcimer and hammered dulcimer, harmonicas and autoharps, old-time music began to take on a genre of its own. The fact that Appalachian music was called by many names shows its diversity. Many of the professionals who played music did not like to be called "hillbilly" musicians. Instead, they chose to call their style "Old Time Country", "Country" or "Mountain Music". It didn't matter when or where they played their music as long as they could play. It is quite common to find Appalachian musicians playing for entertainment and fun at family reunions, and even as a form of spiritual expression at church, "dinners on the ground" and even the old-time tent revivals (Cantwell, 1992).

"Like roads that diverge from the woods, Appalachian music developed its differences around family fireplaces, front porches and barn dances."

The influence of multi-cultures on music was more noticeable during the early stages of Appalachian music. A lot of the fiddle tunes made popular could be traced directly back to the homelands they loved and missed. Every musician of nationality made his or her mark upon the music. Many of the historical tunes on the fiddle show a strong Scotch/Irish influence. Many of the historical styles of the African American banjo tunes are still present in rural Appalachian music. If you were to look at the patterns of Anglo-Celtic music, you would see one identical pattern after another. For many generations, the banjo and fiddle have served as a foundation for every string band in the mountains. So whether you are looking at Monroe's bluegrass music, old-time music, or even the rarely mentioned "Carolina Style" of folk music, Appalachian music has taken on a cultural genre of its own (Wolfe, 1997).

Who were the people that influenced Appalachian music?

Time and space does not permit the listing of a Hall of Fame for Appalachian music. Therefore only a few of the many are mentioned here to give you a flavor of musical history. One of the first great influences I remember growing up is the Carter Family. They are a household staple of those who like the traditional old-time music of the Appalachian area. The Carter family offers us a picture of the typical rural farm family who used their talent and love for music to express life in Appalachia. Their music speaks of those traditional value systems of family honesty, religion and hard work. They carried the image of "old-time musicians" into popularity (Awonitzer, 2002).

If you were to ask, "what is Bluegrass music", the answer would be hard to define. Many people influenced and shaped the music. As with individuality, Bluegrass is as diverse as the people who play it, and the people who identify with its message. Bill Monroe (1911- 1996) and his brothers Charlie and Birch were a strong influence on Bluegrass music. They grew up in the Appalachian county of Ohio, in Kentucky. The brothers began to play music early in life and won the attention of RCA Records. The style of music played by Monroe soon became popular in the mountains. Their group called "The Blue Grass Boys" was actually the root for what was labeled "Bluegrass". Monroe mixed old-time music with blues, rural spiritual songs and even jazz. He was the first in this line of music to make the mandolin popular as a solo instrument (Smith, 2000).

As live radio shows became popular, the old-time music gave way to a new image of "Hillbilly Music". Roy Acuff was a popular singer during the birth of rural mountain music. He was given the nickname "King of the Hillbillies". He sold more records than any other country star during the 1930's and 1940's. Acuff was born in the Appalachian town of Maynardville, Tennessee. An interesting note about Roy Acuff is that he was not just a singer, he was actually a minor league baseball player before he leaned toward music. Although Roy sang a mixture of popular styles of country music laden with traditional sounds, he preferred to play the old hillbilly music. Acuff hit it big when he made popular his songs "The Great Speckled Bird" and "The Wabash Cannonball" (Kinsbury, 1995).

We can't talk about the people or things that molded our old-time, hillbilly or even modern country music without mentioning the influence and stage life of the Grand Ole Opry. I have had occasion to visit the Opry as a child, a teenager and an adult. As I sat there on all three occasions, I couldn't help but soak in the lifestyle of which it spoke. Like kids at Disney World, people sat in awe at the stage presence of "stars" of hillbilly and country music. The Opry is an American original. It began as a radio and stage show with it's first broadcast in 1925. It first aired as a program called the WSM Barn Dance. WSM was a local radio station in Nashville, Tennessee. It became so popular that the station began to invite live audiences into the studio. In 1927, the show assumed the new name and began hiring professional musicians in 1930. Those mentioned already were among the first to take the stage in Nashville (Kinsbury, 1995). The popularity of music in Nashville launched the careers of many and influenced an entire culture. The rest is history.

"Appalachia is ablaze with the sound of music. From the front porch to the big stage, mountain music was born by generations destined to express themselves."

The rich gift of dance

If you stay around Appalachia very long you may be invited "up the ridge" for a Bluegrass show. Just four miles from my home at the Rattlesnake Ridge Community Center in Kentucky, you will find rich mountain music and family string bands. But you will also find DANCE. The young and old both love to dance. At a Bluegrass show you may find some doing a square dance. You may find cloggers doing what they do best. You may find them dancing in groups or dancing alone. A line dance or two will come up during the evening. And then there will be the individual who chooses to do his or her own creative dance. What that dance is.... nobody knows.

"What we do know about the mountain dance is that it is an expression of a joy within. The joy of expression is what makes Appalachian dance unique. Like its music, the gift of dance is a crayon box of joyful expression."

This attempt at looking to the roots of Appalachian dance is only a shaving off of the crayon. To understand the dance of Appalachia, we need to take a quick look at the history of the Irish dance and the Celtic people for they are the strongest influential factor to our dance today. A Celtic people, known as the Gaels, covered Western Europe, the British Isles and parts of Ireland. They all spoke a common language (Gaelic), but they also had another thing in common. They all had a love for music and dance. Although the Roman and Germanic nations subdued the Gaels in most places except Ireland, they could not quench the music and dance of the Gaelic culture. It remained strong. Not much history was kept on music and dance of the Gaelic culture until a few hand written pieces and choreographies on dances were found in the middle 1500's. Political strife during the 1600's and 1700's between the Irish and English saw the culture, customs and commerce of the Irish silenced by Penal Law. Although their expression of music and dance was out of the public eye, it was not absent in the heart of the people.

The controlling English Government allowed limited dancing and musical expression as long as it was part of celebration or ceremony. So, the Gaelic people took every opportunity for celebration and ceremony. As dance became more "allowed" and accepted under English rule, professional Dance Masters became popular in Ireland. A dance master would travel from village to village, teaching as they went. Over the years, a sort of rivalry began between villages. This was what I like to call a showdown-hoedown. In non-Appalachian terms it would be called a dance competition.

This was the birth of dance troupes, competitions and the opening of dance studios across the Irish countryside, similar to our Arthur Murrey studios of the mid 1900's. The addition of costumes that identified them to a troupe, village or clan was common as the individuality of dance emerged. It didn't take long for the Irish dance to take wings and fly across the waters to the Americas where it developed into a style of its own (Breathnach, 1977).

As dance developed in America, it moved from tabletops to stages. It traveled from the fields, barns, and pub cellars of Ireland to public competitions and stage shows. It came to America and took on new forms and new names. Some claim the Irish dance as their father. Included in that family tree would be such American styles as clog dancing in Appalachia, the square dance and other forms of line dancing. Clogging in America, as a folk dance, developed a strong flavor in the southern Appalachian Mountains. Although many may lay claim to influencing clogging in America, I believe one of the greatest influences to the dance we hold dear is the step dance from Ireland and the British Isles. If you watch closely, the clog dance also bears a resemblance to some of the traditional Native American dances. We also see the influence of African Americans in many of our Appalachian clog dances with some still being called Buck Dancing. One of the favorite pass times of early African Americans in the US was to challenge each other in a friendly, free style percussion dance where one may try to out dance the other. That type of "dance challenge" permeated much more of the dance world and is still alive today (Epstein, 1981).

The Appalachian style of clogging is one of the less formal of the styles of folk dance. It is a fun-filled frolic. Usually, it is an individual style of dance where a person free-style dances with as much creativity as possible. This style of dance is very "married" to live string bands, Bluegrass music and old-style music. Also called "mountain dancing", this is the style of clogging you will see on the ridges and in the hollows of Appalachia. It is not unusual at all for someone to stand up at a Bluegrass show and begin to clog. The roots of clogging may be a formal dance, but its style and expression are as personal as they come (Spalding, 1995).

Precision/Modern clogging is a second style of dance that grew in popularity around World War II. Said to be an offspring style of the Irish dance, precision/modern clogging is characterized by line formations, same step dancing, precise choreography, and artistic formations. You can see the similarities between this more formal type of dance and its influence from Celtic and African American dance. One difference found in Precision/Modern clogging is that it sometimes includes dancing to forms of music other than mountain music.

Square Dancing is the Great Grandchild of what is called Contra Dancing. The contra dance can be traced back to England and is unique because it puts dancers in elongated or circular formations. What does Contra mean? It is an abbreviated word for "contrary".

This type of dance places dancers in opposite or "contrary" places where they perform the identical same moves. The formation of squares in dancing styles can be traced to France where they converted equestrian military "quad-drills" into formations on a dance floor. The suggestions have been made that the French merged the long dance of the English with theirs to create a square pattern of dancing. It is no stretch of the imagination to believe the country line-dance of today is influenced by the contra dance. The only difference, so to speak, is that country line-dancers are not "contrary" in position and all face the same direction working in sync like clockwork. It wasn't until the late 50's that modern western square dancing went away from contras in lieu of choreographic routines (Tolman, 1976).

"Dance is one of the many enriching activities that has made Appalachia unique and diverse. To know the dance is to know the people. To watch the dance is to gain a new insight into the culture."

Arts and crafts in Appalachia

Our society looks at Appalachia and recognizes that there is a rich treasure in the arts, crafts and the traditions of yesteryears. The artifacts you may see in craft stores, gift shops, and flee markets across the region are more than just souvenirs. They are replicas of years past. They represent a culture of people who were creative out of necessity. In modern society, Appalachia has become a quaint community with a folk image centered on the art and crafts found in furnishings, tools, instruments, toys and other hand-made necessities. Those necessities are now quaint novelties. The industrial world has missed out on the quality of "craft" by trading the handmade for the impersonal production of goods on the factory line. What modern craft and art lack is that personal touch of true craftsmanship. Appalachian art and crafts were not produced to be art and crafts. They were simple items used out of a necessity for survival on the frontier.

Basket making and weaving were learned to make products for use in everyday life. Pottery wasn't made to sit on the shelf. It was made for daily use. Learning how to make tools from natural materials such as rock and flint meant success or failure in the wild. Candles made at home shed light on a world without electricity. Brooms used in early years were made skillfully out of raw materials from the mountains. Raising sheep for wool and turning raw materials into clothes wasn't a novelty; it was a necessity. Woodworking was not to adorn quaint homes; it had to be learned for building and furnishing the home. Those homes contained beds to sleep on, thus the tick mattresses and feather pillows became a necessity. Quilts were not for hanging on rods in the family room; they were for warming the home and body on cold winter nights. Soap making was passed down from family to family. Children were amused with the crude dolls and toys. Primitive though they may have been, the Appalachian mountain family could not have survived without knowing how to hunt, fish and cook in the wilderness. And let's not forget the practice of free trade in what developed into our modern day flea markets. All of these were a matter of survival. Simply allow a crafter or artist to step out their back door and they can turn a prickly thorn into a Picasso.

"It would be safe to say that as society accepted our "necessities" as "novelties" the creativity of the Appalachian crafter and artist exploded creating a revival of sorts for the culture."

Basket making and weaving

Baskets were a staple item on the Appalachian frontier. They were not decorations that you kept on the counter or threw parties to sell. They were made to use in every day life. Their use included food storage, collecting nuts and berries, storing clothes and even carrying water by adding pine pitch or bear grease. The talent of weaving was used for other purposes such as making sleeping mats, clothing, hats, belts, hammocks and more. The early settlers used a variety of materials for making their day-to-day use baskets (Irwin, 1982).

From the first nation's people, the Appalachians learned to use natural dyes from the forest to help make colorful designs in their woven garments. Some of the materials they used to weave included willow whips, cattails, bulrushes, evergreen needles, barks, long grasses, palm leaves, vines, hemp or corn husks. Finger weaving was also a rural craft passed on through the ages that used leather, twine, yarn, jute, long grasses, inner bark of trees, corn husks, yucca, and hemp to make smaller items such as bracelets, necklaces, headbands, toys, brooms, mops and other small useful items. Weaving became a necessity of sorts to the Appalachian people (Allen, 1970).

"Out of necessity, they learned to use what little they had to create a quality of life. Isn't that what social work is all about: creating quality of life? Something as simple as weaving made their everyday life tolerable."

Pottery in early Appalachia

Stop at any flea market or novelty shop in Appalachia and you will find handmade clay pottery formed in just about any shape imaginable. Clay is found in great quantity in the Appalachian area. You only have to go digging around in old streambeds to find the rich clay used to make our unique forms of art. Dug from around the streams, the rich clay is mixed with other ingredients such as sand, shells, ash or other materials. The clay is then pounded into a fine powder to mix for use.

The early settlers and American Indians used small depressions in the rock in which to grind the clay into a very dry, fine and workable powder. The rest of the process was easy. Water was added to the clay powder and a type of dough made for molding. In Appalachia, the first Americans made their pottery into cone-shaped bowls using a style called the coil process. It reminds me of the "snakes" we made as a child with modeling clay. We would role the clay between our hands as fast as we could to make long roles and then create "clay art" projects. Though simple it sounds, this is the same process used to form their earliest pots and bowls. A simple and effective technique used by early potters was to start with a large ball of clay, put a fist into the middle and shape it until you had the bowl shaped the way you wanted (Wigginton, 1984).

A third and final technique of making pottery was slab sculpting. This is a more creative style, which allows the sculptor to carve and form the clay into unique shapes and patterns. The decoration of the pottery is what made Appalachian pottery unique. Potters often carve or scratch their design into the pottery while it is still damp. Some more creative artists use leaves and grass to create fossil designs and nature's patterns. To harden their works of art they would fire it in an open pit (Guilland, 1971).

Though creative and beautiful, the pots created in early Appalachian history were made of necessity. A family couldn't survive without pots to store food, carry water, eat and drink from and even cook upon. For the rural family, the making of pottery was a necessity for living. If you ever have an opportunity to observe the making of pottery, stop and enjoy the craft. It will give you a good touch with the past.

The art of flint knapping to create tools

Flint knapping is a novelty you may see demonstrated at many a state park or re-enactment in Appalachia. Flint knapping was something most frontiersmen learned in order to make it in the wild. What is it? It is the making of stone and bone weapons, tools and useful instruments. The most common material used was a creek cobblestone. With a little work and patience, creek cobblestones were chipped to make knives, axes, hoes and other tools. John Shadow Eagle, a close friend of Native American Heritage, visited my children often and shared with them the art of making arrowheads from flint found in these Appalachian Mountains. One of his handmade bows with flint tipped arrows hangs proudly in my office as does a deer antler handled knife. He tells of how his people would trade with other tribes for copper to make striking stones or billets for flint knapping. To make a copper striking stone, they would first take a stick and make a hole in the ground about six inches deep by one inch wide. They would melt the copper and pour it into the holes to cool. Once cooled, they would remove the now solid copper striking stone to use in flint knapping. Other tools they used to make flint items were things such as deer antlers and billets made from moose antlers traded for with other tribes. The ideal types of cobbles used to knap were flint, chert, quartz, ryolite and obsidian. The early Indians and settlers found their best knaps in caves throughout the hills of Appalachia. Over the years, the tradition of knapping was refined and passed down from century to century. All those who learned the art did so out of necessity. In a modern society, there is no need for tools of flint and stone (Tolman, 1976). Very few still practice the art, but those that do, help to keep the memory of this Appalachian practice alive. If you search the soils of farms in the area, you can still find arrowheads of flint.

Candle making

Carrying on a tradition from English ancestors, candle making was another art learned and passed on out of necessity and survival. In Europe, the usual source of light for common folk was called a rushlight. It was made of a reed stripped to its pith and soaked in oil. The tallow and beeswax candles were very popular to both make and use. The beeswax candles were costly and usually used by the upper Colonial society. The tallow candles were called "dips" because they were dipped in suet or hard fat from animals and then used to provide light in the home. The wicks of these early candles were made from flax or cotton yarn. The wicks we use today are made of woven cotton treated with mineral salts. In the mountains, if a family wanted candles they had to make them. They would cut a wick the exact length wanted and hang them from a frame above a tub of melted wax. The wicks would then be dipped into the wax over and over with intervals of time to give the wax time to cool. The process continued until the candle reached the right thickness. After formed, the candle was smoothed and finished. Beeswax candles were made in a similar way, but the wax was dripped over the wick instead of being dipped. Most beeswax candles were saved and used for very special social events or in religious services.

In the 1850's, paraffin wax was discovered and it became the common source for "city made candles". You don't have to look far anywhere in the United States to find candles made in a variety of aromas, styles, jars and decorative containers. It is a "new" popular hobby for many. In an attempt to make a home today look and smell rustic, homemakers have revived the art of candle making. Candles now adorn and decorate almost every home or church. Although a decorative piece today, the story of candles speaks of a time when a mountain family could not survive without them.

Broom and brush making

Hand crafted brooms and brushes have become a very unique novelty craft in Appalachia. Most brooms of yesteryear were made from the tops of broomcorn plants. Almost all brooms today are made by machinery. In early Appalachia, broom makers had to use the crudest of instruments to make their wares. They would first take the dried tops of the broomcorn plant and attach them to a wooden stick. Sometimes it was a tree limb or "whittled to suit" handle. It was usually attached by winding staging wire around the broomcorn to secure it to its handle. Some people liked the cone-shaped bundle of straws just the way they were. It was easier to get into corners when the broom was straight. To get the shape we currently have for brooms, the cone-shaped broomcorn was put in a vise, flattened, and sewed with heavy twine to hold it in shape. The final touches were made to the broom by scraping off the broomcorn seeds still attached to the fibers. The end of the broom was then trimmed even and ready for use (Olney, 2002).

When it came to making smaller hand brooms, brushes and paintbrushes, they often chose hog bristle as material. Because hog hair bristles split at the end and were somewhat bushy, they were ideal for paintbrushes. Even today some of the work of making paintbrushes is done by hand. As you travel throughout Appalachia, you will still find "home made" brooms in novelty shops and state parks. The next time you pick one up, think about the rich heritage of the Appalachian people.

Clothing: from wool to wardrobe

In the history of our Appalachian ancestors, raising sheep for wool to make yarn was about as important as raising stock and animals for food. Today, there are not many who still raise sheep to make their own yarn. In some "preserved" museums or recreated villages, there are people who still know the process. Heavy industry has swallowed up the making of wool garments, but the sheep farmer still supplies the wool needed. Sheep were hard to come by in Appalachia. Most people guarded their flocks carefully. They were hard to buy in the settlement years, especially during winter and cold months. Almost everyone had sheep. If a family didn't have one, a relative would willingly share any surplus wool. Sheep were usually sheared once per year in the spring and sometimes in early fall to allow the sheep to build up warmth for the winter months. Depending on the size of the sheep, they would produce 1 to 2 ½ pounds of wool. Once the wool was cut, washed, dried, carded (the process of breaking up the wool and getting it ready to spin), combed, and put upon a roll, they were taken to the spinning wheel where they were spun tightly into wool strings or yarn (Goodrich, 1989).

The early mountain people had to rely upon natural dyes if they were to add color to their clothing. They would use plants boiled down in iron pots. The wool skeins would then be added to the dye mixture. The skeins were then hung, sun dried or air-dried until time to weave on the loom. The Appalachians were very skilled at weaving on looms. The personality, pattern and even family tradition was exhibited in each original creation.

Spinning and weaving was a daily routine for Appalachian women, but has become a novelty and a retro experience over the years for those who delve back into Appalachian history. One issue usually not mentioned about this type of daily activity for families is that spinning and weaving were often a social event participated in by family and even community.

> *"What does this have to do with social issues? As in most "necessity" activities, living in Appalachia meant group cooperation, sharing and socializing. Spinning and weaving was one of the most cherished 'social' activities of the Appalachian community."*

Woodwork: survival not souvenir

To the hills of the Appalachian Mountains, the settlers brought very little but themselves and a few crude tools. What they did bring was a lot of creativity. That creativity made it easy to learn the art of woodwork and tool making. Wood was of course easily accessible and the most viable solid material on the frontier. Therefore, most of their tools were made from wood. Most all tools had wooden handles of various types of solid wood. Mallets, mauls, and wooden wedges were made from small and large hardwood trees of oak, hickory, or white oak saplings (Hodges, 1964).

> *"This natural resource of the mountains became the resource of survival for its people. The tools and items made from wood often determined the way of life for the self-sufficient mountain family."*

Whether for work or shelter, the role wood played in the settling of the Southern Appalachians is vital. Today wood is seen as a garnish or trim to add to the "country" or "rustic" look of a building. For our ancestors, it provided fire for warmth and cooking, shelter from weather, material for furniture and utensils, wagons, wheels, tools, homes, shingles, barns, buckets, barrels and fence posts. All of these were made and used to etch out a living in the mountains. Only until the modernization of metal and iron did this "art" fade away. Even with the modernization of mills and such, wood was and is still a source of necessity for the Appalachian people (Christensen, 1952).

Not all woodwork in Appalachia was limited to the building of necessary items from wood. At folk art festivals and nostalgic museums you will see the artistic work of many of the Appalachian woodcarvers. Ornate walking sticks, statues, wood-burned plagues, and other woodcarvings found in the Appalachian area are much like the ornate work many of the immigrants did in their homelands. The woodwork you will find in Appalachia is very distinct, and you are liable to find it anywhere. Even in our own quaint little town, you can see the original handiwork of local woodcarvers on our roadsides. Appalachia is ablaze with the creativity of its people.

Beds and pillows

Our Appalachian ancestors did not have the luxury of fine beds with spring mattresses. As a teenager, I remember a song by John Denver, which reminded me of my visits to Grandma Yorke's house. The song was titled "Grandma's Feather Bed". People of the mountain crafted their beds annually. Some beds and pillows weren't so comfortable, but each family made their mattresses and pillows from the materials they had. Picture an early settler making a mattress and pillow for their bed. By trial and error, a person was not always satisfied with the comfort it lacked. You can imagine what types of conversations and complaints one may have heard at that time. I can also hear the reply that must have come:

"'You've made your bed, now lie in it!' This is not the only colloquialism that originated in Appalachian culture."

The mattress and pillows were a simple sack made of whatever material was available to the family. Time would be spent making a wood frame from the crude or even finished lumber available. That crafted frame was equipped with corded or rope netting that was weaved together to form a hammock of sorts. The bed sack was then filled with straw or hay and their pillows were made from feathers collected from the fowl or poultry on the farm. To have a bed sack made of feathers was a luxury on the frontier and very rare. To complete the bed, the straw or feather bed sack was laid on top of the corded bed frame. How did they "freshen up" their mattresses? The straw beds were emptied each year and sometimes even washed, dried and then reused. The straw "tick" bed on a wooden frame was very typical of the Appalachian and frontier home (Dane, 1990). Also typical was the family quilt that decorated them. Perhaps tonight when you decide to 'hit the hay' you may remember the originality of the Appalachian straw tick bed.

Quilting

Like a swarm of bees stinging in harmony, the quilting needle never stopped at a "quilting bee" until the quilt was done. A quilting bee was a gathering of friends who came together to make quilts. I remember my grandmother talking about going quilting and trading patterns with family and friends. Most of all, I remember those cold Christmas nights sleeping at Grandma's house under quilts so heavy you couldn't move. The quilts they made had patterns of every size and shape. The patterns were endless: Wedding Rings, Odd Fellows, Rocky Road, Nine Diamonds, Attic Window, Trip Around the Mountain, Monkey Wrench, Drunkards Path, Four Doves at the Well, Little Dutch boy or girl, Double T, Friendship and a variety of other popular patterns. Some say the rise in interest today in quilting has to do with the nostalgia of craft. The social impact of this social activity speaks loudly of family, of friends and the simple times when people once built relationships around quilting.

"I have been looking at life through systems theory too long to not see the social strength of such an activity. Other than church and barn-raising, there is not another activity in Appalachian history that was more social oriented than quilting."

Besides the craft itself, years of custom and tradition surrounded the making of quilts. Patterns for quilts were like trading baseball cards today. They were traded, given away and even shown off at local and state fairs. The patterns (much like the clan pattern of clothes in Celtic tradition) often handed down a family legacy or tradition. Grandmothers would often make a quilt for every grandchild. In our home, we still have quilts made by Grandma. I remember this tradition from my childhood. Grandma used all those colloquial sayings like: 'If a young lady sleeps under a new quilt she will dream of the man she will marry." It was around those quilting bees that folktales and "old wives tales" grew. To host a quilting bee meant an all day social time (Atkins, 1994). The person who invited friends over for the quilting bee was asking friends to help her make or finish the quilt for herself or her family. They would provide breakfast, lunch and even dinner if needed until the quilt was completed. Often they would come together to make a quilt for a needy family or as a wedding present for a young couple. They would work until their quilt or even two were done (Ferrero, 1987).

"Gone are the days of the quilting bee, but the quilt as an art form is still alive. It is not unusual to go into 'societies finest' homes and businesses and see the quality of a fine quilt hanging on display. The art is not lost."

What in blazes is a flea market?

The flea market reigns supreme in Appalachia. The flea market is a unique mountain event. It is a phenomenon that is no longer just a cultural event. It is a nationwide pass time. The flea market was the brainchild of those who bartered and traded on the early frontier. It was a social event where people would trade their dogs, cattle, horses, farm animals, crops or other homemade arts and crafts. No one loved to trade coon dogs and knives more than my grandfather John. Although he passed away when I was young, I remember him showing off knives and guns he had traded. I pass several flea market sites daily, and sometimes I can't fight the urge to stop to see what "deals" I can find. Can you finish this line: "One man's trash is another man's _____." Treasure of course! Today you will find "flea markets" on every highway and byway of our nation. Invariably you will find groups of "locals" hovered around the tailgate of a friend. Their social bond is evident as they spin tales of old fishing trips, childhood and the "good-ole-days". Friendships are built and goods are traded. It is a micro system within a macro system of economy.

"Now an American tradition, the flea market speaks strong of the free trade system established in our nation. It is a place where one man's discard becomes another man's jewel. Nowhere will you find this practice more alive than in Appalachia."

How does this relate to social work in Appalachia?

I can answer that question by sharing one of my most vivid home visits. My visit to family "A" was like a blast to the past. Primitive living was what they called it. I called it poverty. Yet, the children were clean and the "primitive" dwelling lacked any sign of electricity, water or modern heating system. It was clean nevertheless. A handmade axe and old time saw sat used on the porch. Homemade quilts covered the windows to keep out the cold. Candles were placed strategically around the room for light. A "pot-bellied" stove sat in the middle of the dwelling for warmth and cooking. A beat-up ice cooler held the babies milk. A homemade basket in the corner held the family Bible and family picture album. You could tell the basket had had many practical uses in its day. Handmade doilies were on the table in front of me and crafted afghans lined the couch I sat upon. A set of hand carved, wood "praying hands" were the items that book-ended Granny's worn Bible. This type of simple life is not uncommon in Appalachia. If you want a glimpse of a unique culture as a social worker, simply venture into the hollows of my Eastern Kentucky hills. There you will find what you seek. What is found in this study is a short look at the old ways of life.

> *"Although knowledge of the old ways of daily living may not target social reform, the knowledge you receive will give you insight into the culture of Appalachia. It will help you prepare for work with those who still live a primitive life in the Appalachians. For them, it is not just a way of life. It is a way of survival."*

Why so much focus on these simple ways of life?

We call them simple ways of life, but they were not so simple. They were a means of survival. Their life experiences taught them to be creative and innovative out of necessity. Only to a society who passed them by are they quaint and rustic. Time and page limitations do not permit me to detail the history of all our Appalachian practices. I write of them because we often forget the hardships our ancestors faced as they attempted to survive the wilderness.

Another reason I write of them is that we often forget our roots. We turn on the imitation gas logs in our fireplace instead of having to go out to the woodpile and cut our own logs. There are children and adults in our nation today that have never been on a farm, never milked a cow nor collected eggs for their own breakfast. They have never used an outhouse or read from an oil lamp.

> *"We often forget the struggles that paved the way for the comfortable existence in which we now live. We tend to romanticize the history of our people. However, many of our Appalachian people are still stuck in time."*

Often, we take for granted the simplest commodities. Many of the luxuries of life like soap, water and warm blankets under which to sleep are still nonexistent for many families in the mountains and foothills of Appalachia. As you read this book, you may be sitting in a nice home, a modular dwelling, an apartment or dorm room. One of my children tonight will come home to macaroni and cheese. She won't be able to read the title of this book. She will curl up to sleep tonight on a tattered quilt in the corner of a shack that she calls home. And she will be happy for what she has.

These few inclusions of music, art and the making of items crucial to life in the early Appalachian hills, gives us only a brush with our Appalachian roots. Understanding these ways of life help us understand the social lifestyle of a forgotten culture. Why is it so important? The bottom line is this:

"The Roots of Appalachian music and art are truly an expression of our culture. Whether you are working with children, adults or families in Appalachia now or are simply studying the culture, you will find they are not so far removed from the past and the old ways of life. This trip to the past helps us identify with their present."

CHAPTER SEVEN

SELF-DETERMINATION, INDEPENDENCE, AND PRIDE:

The cornerstones of social life in Appalachian culture

Any Social Worker's approach to practice is going to be unique to them. However, there are some general practices that are universal. That is why the National Association of Social Workers wrote our code of ethics. That code greatly influences our ethical responsibility to clients. It provides us with guidelines for meeting the most important needs of our children and families.

"Three of the most important characteristics I have found common in working with the Appalachian people are self-determination, independence and pride."

Many authors have written about Appalachia and most all are in agreement that these characteristics are strong in the foothills of our great region. The challenge in social work is to learn how to harness these wonderful qualities for goodness of fit.

Self-determination in Appalachia

My definition of self-determination is **"the ability to make ones own decisions concerning fate, destiny and direction in life"**. When I think of this foundational social concept, I see self-determination as synonymous with decision-making. In the real world, decision-making ranks right up there with basic human rights. The whole premise of addressing self-determination in the Social Worker's Code of Ethics was to encourage us to protect the rights of individuals to make decisions about their own fate, destiny, and direction in life.

"In my opinion, one of the most important goals in social work is helping clients make independent decisions and determinations that will bring them quality of life."

The history of this great country rests on the premise that we are an independent nation, established for the freedom of the people. Wars have been fought to protect our right to self-determination. As mentioned before, this search for freedom of choice was a drawing factor for those who sought a new land of opportunity and for those who longed for the right to live as they chose to! This idea of self-determination, provided to all under the Constitution of the United States of America, has been the greatest drawing factor for our country. The rural areas of Appalachia are even more alluring to those drawn to a secluded lifestyle. Not a finer example of self-determination could be found than in Appalachia. Travel into the backwoods and "hollers" and you will find a culture of people who take great joy in their freedom of self decision-making. For years, the mountain people have chosen their own way of life. They have never marched to the beat of someone else's drum. They are thankful for the freedom to decide where and how they will live. The strong self-determination of the Appalachian people could be seen both in a positive and negative light.

On the positive side, self-determination is a strong characteristic that holds a family together. And it is usually that self-determined family who rises above the stereotype of the culture. An individual who makes right decisions about their destiny and direction has taken charge of their own life. You will find this strength within the mountain people. On the negative side, self-determination can also be a weak characteristic that holds a person to a wrong course of life. Stubbornness may be a better term to describe self-determination gone wrong. I have worked with multi-generations of families stuck in the cycle of poverty and destructive lifestyles of their own choosing. Even when provided with a plan, program or means to rise above their situation they exercise their right to stay defeated (Deci, 1985).

"Self-determination can provide goodness of fit or lack of fit. Our role as a social worker can make all the difference in the world. It is up to us to learn how to work with this strong and proud people."

Independence: a strong Appalachian quality

The Appalachian people are an independent people. They honor this above most all things! Their independence is an admirable characteristic. During the floods and storms of April 1997 and March of 2001 in Eastern Kentucky, my staff and I began to do flood relief work in our small rural town. The only federal housing project within 15 miles had lost 24 of its 28 apartment units to flooding. The apartments were filled with at least three feet of water, and when the waters receded there was not much left to salvage. The victims of high water were mainly children with single moms and senior adults who had little or no possessions. What they did have was a proud and independent spirit. For those of us who were there to help them pick up the pieces, it was hard to understand why they initially did not want our help.

Our first relief effort was with a senior adult who had been widowed for years. She had no family. She had no help. As we came to her home, she welcomed us with open arms and a tear in her eyes. The only things we were able to save in her home were her glassware figurines, trinkets that she held dear to her heart and several can food items she had resting on top of her tall cupboard. She had been "saving them for hard times". This was definitely one of those hard times. Instead of taking those goods down to prepare for herself, she replied: "I know of a gentleman one building down who lost everything. I bet he could use some of this food. Why don't you folk go take him that food. I'll be alright." Of course we took care of both of them, but that spirit is the independence of which I speak.

Later that day, we set out to locate one of our single mothers and her children. For two days we tried to catch them to make sure they were alright. Each time we would find an empty apartment not yet touched by any clean up effort. When we finally found them, she and her children had been helping an elderly couple down the road before they tackled their own reality. The mother's response was simply: "We are going to be just fine when this is all over with. We'll get to our place when we can. The kids and I can put the place back together in no time."

This spirit of independence and caring is part of the Appalachian culture. The spirit of independence within our Southern Highland families is often all we have to hold onto. The early pioneers self-determination and independence was a driving force for survival during the hardships they faced. Today, there is a strong pull to think the same way. People in our small backwoods communities still band together. You may be a perfect stranger, but if you have a need you can count on others to give you a hand up when you need it.

The historical practices of barn raisings, crop sharing, and the barter system are still alive and well in the mountains. They are all signs of a people who aren't afraid to get out there and try to make it on their own. It is not unusual, even today, to see lines of cars parked along the side of the road selling garden vegetables, fruits and household items. Industrious people still walk the side roads collecting cans for cash. It is not unusual to see an old flatbed truck loaded with scrap metal going to the recycling bins. The flea market and swap meets are still a major part of life in the mountains. All of this is evidence of people who are willing to "go it on their own". Although this independent spirit is a positive quality, it can also be a detriment to the provision of services by social work professionals. Appalachian people cherish their solitude, and infringements on that privacy are often resented (Fisher, 1993).

"Standing against the status quo is a common part of the culture. Going our own way or blazing our own trail is a mark of the self-determined, independent spirit. It is what we do!"

Whether making our own clothes, raising our own food, supplying our own milk, butter, cheese, sorghum, eggs and meat, building our own homes and furniture, repairing our own cars or making our own instruments, the Appalachian people are satisfied with living our life the way we choose. We are a culture so independent that we would rather suffer in need than ask for help. We would rather stay lost than ask directions. We would rather be wrong than to back down from an opinion, even if we know our opinion is wrong. We would rather do without than accept welfare. The independent spirit of the Appalachian family comes from not having to depend upon others. When it comes to self...we would like to be left alone.

One of the major influences of the Scottish/Irish culture in the mountains was a strong sense of the clan, the family and belonging. This meeting of the clans is still a major emphasis in Ireland and Scotland. When you mention families in Appalachia, you automatically think of large families, reunions and the whole family meeting at grandma's house. During the summer, it's not uncommon to see "Family Reunion" signs dotting the roadways and giving direction to kinfolk coming home for a visit. When the weather is good, on any given Sunday, you can tour the hollows and ridges and see churchyards filled with "Homecoming" festivities and dinner on the grounds. You can drive down any given road or up any mountaintop and see yards full of family. As you pass most homes with a front porch, you can guarantee there will be family sitting there and they will wave as you pass.

Like strong English families rallying around the family crest and coat of arms, Appalachian families hold strong to family ties and genealogies.

The big Hatfield and McCoy family conflict shared in a previous chapter, is a prime example of this strong family bonding. If there were to be a moral to that story, it would be that the sense of family and belonging is thicker than blood. Loyalty to family runs thick. Modern day marriage ceremonies use the vows that promise to love, honor, and cherish through sickness and health, for richer and for poorer. The sense of family in Appalachia has that same strong bond during times of sickness, hard times and even death. The sense of family even reaches to raising children of the extended family. It is not uncommon for families to take in relatives until they can "get on their feet". "Family is family" is what we hear when working with the people of the mountains. This sense of family and belonging is a strength that our nation greatly benefits from. It has once been said: "As the family goes, so goes the nation!"

Appalachian Pride: The issues that both build and shatter pride

Appalachia is a region rich in natural resources. From the rich coalfields to the timber filled mountains, Appalachia is ablaze with "things that build pride". On the flip side, Appalachia has been plagued with "things that shatter pride". Unemployment is one of those plaguing issues. The Appalachian people have always had a strong work ethic. They are a hard working, multi-skilled people. Resilient would be the best word to describe them. Contrary to most stereotypes, the average person in Appalachia is ready and willing to work. They are willing to learn new skills and do what it takes to provide a way of life for themselves and their family. However, the opportunity to etch out a living is not always available (Gaventa, 1990).

Industrial breakthroughs in mining between 1980 and 1990 sent over 84 thousand miners home with pink slips. Unemployment sent them packing to the larger cities and states outside of Appalachia where jobs could be found. The families who chose to stay were left with little or no revenue and a falling infrastructure that has brought the region to its knees. If you talk with people of the mountains about coal mining, logging and industry you might not get a positive response. "They've stripped our land, dug out our mountains, taken our trees and moved on! Our railroads are gone, the brickyards are closed, so what are we suppose to do now?" I receive this response from many of the people I work with in Eastern Kentucky. In the wake of the hard facts, I have to agree that industry has depleted most of the rich resources of our region and left little behind for those who call Appalachia home. The mines are closed. The trees have been harvested. The brickyards are desolate. Why did it happen? When the coal industry and lumbering companies came into Appalachia, their money appealed to a people accustomed to living with very little.

"Those who held the deeds to rich forests and deep veins of coal knew nothing about the great value and wealth that lay beneath their family home places. The idea of being able to put food on the table and clothes on their children seemed, at the time, more important. Their immediate need outweighed the long term outcome. This is still a detrimental social issue today. Many of our people sacrifice the future for the immediate, making unwise decisions that affect the future."

Big Industry held out a carrot stick. One by one, families sold off their rights to wealth. Those that could have been rich mine owners, were destined to be poor coal miners. Those that could have been rich from the harvest of lumber now worked the sawmills located in every hollow available in the mountains. Forced to move off of the land they once owned, they were not left with many options for living. Logging operations in the mountains cleared the trees and left much of the land barren. Because of that, the land held very little value for housing, farming and etching out a living for the family. Travel the back roads through the highlands of Appalachia and you will see ghost towns in areas that were once booming. Now, vacant mine shafts litter the mountainside. In Appalachia today, you will find very few working mines. The coal trucks still roll strong down State Highway 23, but to look at the local economies of the rural region, one couldn't tell. Although sincere attempts at reclamation are being made, I'm afraid the industrial damage is done!

What do I mean by industrial damage? The whole Appalachian culture was placed in the balances and forced to choose options for their life. One side of the scale called for the mountain people to jump on the bandwagon of the "industrial race". The other side of the scale tipped toward the people choosing to make a living raising crops, cattle, logging, trapping for fur or raising grain to use for whiskey. Yes, whiskey! Take a quick side study on the Whiskey Rebellion and you'll find many Appalachian farmers who turned to harvesting grain for the alcohol industry. The sale of Appalachian whiskey was such a popular product that it caused some serious social problems for the new US government under President George Washington. Further, during the Prohibition, you will see the Appalachian states as one of the highest producers of "moonshine" whiskey. But that is a story for another time. In regard to making a living off the land, the land may have been rich yet the people were not. The scales were tipped in favor of the "industrial race" that squeezed out those who chose a different path. Industry had a corner on the market. The Appalachian culture has barely survived the industrial push for success.

"The coalfields brought wealth to the owners, but desolation to the land. The industrial race has in the past and is to this day a trauma for both the people and the mountains. The Appalachian culture is now suffering from what could be called post-traumatic stress of an entire culture, and the trauma continues on!"

The land and forests in the mountains are in slow repair after being desolate and unusable for years. I once visited an elderly gentleman and the conversation led to this very topic. He stated: "The logging that went on when I was a kid was kind of exciting at first, but when the loggers were gone, it looked like locust had come through!" What he meant was this: The large logging camps came into an area, stripped the trees clean and left. He later replied: "The coal camps weren't any better! They'd come in and set up 'little cities', do their business and leave us years latter holding the coal dust!" There were massive migrations of workers into these little coal towns while the mines were rich. The rich resources are now gone, and so are the jobs. The sudden opening and closing of mines were traumatic on the small towns that dotted the Appalachian countryside. As the resources dwindled, so did the communities. It wasn't just the mines that suffered. The stores that once sold goods and groceries now lay in ruin. The churches that once thrived, foster congregations you could count on two hands. Gas stations that pumped thousands of gallons of diesel fuel stand rusted and grown up with weeds. The schools are now closed and playgrounds are empty.

Many chose to follow the mining, but others did no choose the migrant life. Instead, they chose to stay and create a life in the mountains (Haynes, 1997).

Appalachian pride is one thing that keeps many of our families going. When I said resilient before, I meant that though industry had failed, the more resourceful have found ways to provide. They may not have much, but they are proud of what they have. By any measure, the hard work of the average mountain family was and is just enough to survive. The thing that carries them through hard times and depression is their pride and self-determination. Still today, the Appalachian people are a breed of proud, independent and yes, stubborn people. When Lyndon B. Johnson declared war on poverty in the 60's, Appalachia was ground zero. Since then, Government economists have attempted to fix Appalachia with federal billions. Some areas of Appalachia have jumped on the victory wagon, but others have fallen off. The economic prosperity of some communities speaks highly of Government efforts. Other communities are war zones, and they hold their prisoners of war hostage. My community is one such victim of the poverty war. You can see the casualties everywhere. The average school in my region sees 70-80% of its children living under the poverty level and relying on the governmental free and reduced lunch programs for what may be the only meals they receive. One can not be blind to the fact that there are many such non-rural communities across America who suffer the same plight of their children. However, in Appalachia it is a poverty that wears a different coat. The plight of most social workers in rural America is not that the helping agencies have run out of funding to help those in need. Our plight is that there are not resources to begin with. Ways to help our families are often non-existent. The hardest thing I have had to do in practice is to look into a crying young mother's eyes and say: "I am so...so...sorry! I have exhausted every resource that is available and I am not going to be able to help you." Those times for a professional always make us feel helpless. But it is also those times that validate our choice of the right career.

"The concept that most of society doesn't yet acknowledge is that you can't fix the poor. You can give them a hand up, the resources (if available) to provide and the means to succeed. After that, the poor must also take responsibility and pull themselves up by the bootstrap."

Poverty is a powerful social issue in Appalachia. Let me share. One day in practice, I began a journey to visit one of my children. I traveled a four-lane highway passing modern hotels along the way. The four-lane highway took me to a two-lane State road. That State road leads to a ridge road that winds around what many call Mountain Top Road. I make a stop on that two-lane road to turn up a "holler". There in the middle of nowhere is a mansion fit for a king. You thought I was going to talk about poverty didn't you. The story doesn't end there. Keep traveling up the "holler" where the nice blacktop ends in a gravel road. Keep traveling up the gravel road where it ends in a dirt road. Keep traveling up the dirt road where it ends on a creek bed. Keep traveling up the creek bed where you will find a grassy pasture. You've arrived in true Appalachia. There in a pasture sits an old rusted, broken down school bus. It doesn't transport children anymore, but it does house a grandmother, two adults, a 17 year-old single mother and three beautiful children. I asked once what brought them to this place. The answer was: "This was where our old home place was year ago. We were all raised here. The land has been in our family for years."

As I looked up, I saw the children come running around the side of the bus jumping up and down, hollering: "We got company!!!!". It's hard to say why they seemed to be happy even though they were living in poverty. The grandma met me with a howdy! The children laughed and played in the dirt pile while mom and I talk about their truancy. I looked beyond their matted, lice-filled hair, through the grime on their little faces, and tooth decayed smiles to realize: "this is what social work is about". The children jumped into my arms for a big hug before I left, and I embraced them willingly! "We get to come to school tomorrow if mommy can get these bugs out of our hair!" As I went to get into my car, the youngest was already sitting in the passenger seat. With big brown eyes searching, the child asks: "Can I go home with you?" A professional cannot have experiences like this without being touched. From that day on in practice, I signed all my letters: "For the Children".

"I wonder...is this the way their life will always be? Do they want any better for themselves? Will poverty always loom at their front door? Can we empower them for change?"

In reality, these precious children don't know they are living in poverty. This is all the life they know. Great-Grandma lived in a shack at the back of the holler. Grandma built a lean-to onto her place. Mommy had the initiative to drive in a big yellow school bus for them to live in! Never mind the fact they have no water and the same old outhouse has served the family for years. Ever so often they build a new one to replace the old. They feel grateful that their kerosene heater is still working (their only source of heat during the winter). Dad made the statement to me: "I bet you don't see people live this primitive anymore, do you?" Sadly, I do see families who live that way on a daily basis. I struggle daily with the poverty in Appalachia. One of the hardest things about working in rural America without funding is to have to daily search without success for the resources to empower your clients. It is hard to tell your clients: "I don't have the resources to help you and your family right now." I'm sorry doesn't feed the hungry, clothe the naked or keep their water and electric turned on. With limited resources, we do all we can for children and families! **Until you actually experience Appalachia like this, you won't understand the people who live here. That is the real purpose of this book. I want to give you a glimpse, so please look deep!**

The unemployment rate in our region for those who are the head of a household brings major cause for concern. Being able to provide for your family should be a source of pride. I found this more so in the Appalachians. I have heard some of my dads say: "A man ain't a man if he can't take care of his family. I don't need no welfare!" What he does want though is "workfare".

He wants to work, but can't find it. The cost of unemployment is not only measured in the form of money. It is also measured in human emotions. Regardless of where you live, being unable to provide the bear necessities of life for the family has happened to most every husband or father at some time in life. Not being able to provide is a jolt to your pride. One of my fathers put it this way: "Not being able to bring home the bacon means you're a failure to your family." In a culture where a man's value is placed on how he provides for the family, the feelings of failure and inadequacy are pretty hard to carry. Enter depression, followed by the multiple fallout of social problems to the family.

"This plane of mental perception is where my Appalachian families live. This is a life situation that can shatter the pride of any individual who is trying to do their best for the family."

Living from small paycheck to small paycheck, families have learned to squeeze every penny to provide the basics. It always seems to be harder as fall comes and the seasonal unemployment nightmare converges on a large number of rural families. With the small bit of industry we do have, the seasons of work are slow. Construction jobs come to a halt. Weather hinders the work at the sawmill. Farming is limited to seasons. Other outdoor work almost halts during winter. If there are jobs available in rural Appalachian communities, they are family businesses or part-time minimum wage service positions. Approximately 80% of the jobs in our small county are with the local school system. The county in which we live doesn't even have an unemployment office. What jobs are available? They are service-oriented or fast food positions. However, teenagers who are energetic and will work anytime for any wage are usually the ones to first fill the vacancies. What is the result? The "bread winner" or single mom who is trying to make it must head to the unemployment line 30-45 miles away. What is the outcome? There is little hope of success.

Legislators and Community officials often do their best to bring industry to rural Appalachia. However successful they may be with bringing in high tech industry, we still have a dilemma. We have no infrastructure to support it! Even if we did, most of those available jobs require high levels of education and technical skill. The average laborer in Appalachia doesn't have the technical training or education to step into such a quality job. Building a supportive infrastructure in Appalachia has been a long, hard fight. There have been some wonderful success stories in parts of the mountains. We stand in hope that "the powers that be" continue addressing the issues that have left our culture behind.

To be conscious of these few but powerful social issues that drive the trials of Appalachian families is to gain a better understanding of social work with a self-determined, independent and proud people. There have been many times at home when I have reached for a hammer to put a screw into a wall. I have used an adjustable wrench as a hammer because it was close. After all, it was the tool I used successfully on the last job I did. Just because it worked for me on the last job, doesn't mean it will work on the job at hand.

Social work is much the same way. We all have favorite tools we use with clients that are successful. And because they are successful, we tend to use them over and over again with those in our care. We, therefore, take those same therapeutic tools out for use with diverse clients for their interventions. Folks, it just doesn't work that way! The bottom line is this:

"Social issues with rural, suburban and urban cultures may often be the same, but you can not always use the same tool for successful intervention. Social work practice is diverse. Learn about Appalachia, and you will learn about the cornerstones of social life within it."

CHAPTER EIGHT

APPALACHIAN HUMOR OR HUMOR ABOUT APPALACHIA:

A look at humors impact upon a culture

Proverb 17 says: "a merry heart is as good medicine." Laughter is a healing balm for the mind, body and soul. When people are at their worse, it is then they need laughter the most. There is a difference, however, between targeted humor and the use of humor to help you through! One of the strengths of the Appalachian people is the ability to laugh at self. Humor is also a great defense mechanism many people use to keep themselves sane in an insane world. If you can laugh at yourself and your plight in life, it may just be an avenue of empowerment (Billings, 2001).

There is no one who enjoys laughter more than myself. We have a plaque in our home that says: "Live well! Laugh often! And Love much!" Laughter is a standard in our home. Spending my younger years outside of Appalachia, it wasn't uncommon to hear "Kentuckian" jokes. There is not a week that passes that I don't get a redneck or hillbilly email from one of my friends "up North", and they do bring a smile or two. Here's the question. Where do you draw the line when a joke that gets a thousand laughs is done at the expense of someone else's life style? Why is it that some may laugh and some may not? Could it be that the jokes are truer of their physical or economic make-up than they are just funny? Are they stereotypical? Are they in bad taste? You decide.

Let me be honest and say that humor about culture and in this case "hillbilly humor" is not always in bad taste, nor is it always offensive. As many comedians say: "It depends on who's telling the joke whether it's funny or not!" Why do you think people of different races, religions, minorities and cultures tell jokes about themselves? It is because life is humorous and laughter often is a good cover for coping with reality.

"Even in life's worse situations, laughter can help to ease the pure reality of pain. Laughter is not going to make our troubles go away, but it makes those tough life situations a little more bearable. How would you color life? Life in Appalachia is quite like a box of crayons. We may choose to color with broken shades of black and gray, or we can pull out the brightest and the best to color our life with joy and laughter. Blazing colors and vibrant hues are what characterize our strong and proud mountain culture!!"

Where does humor cross the line and when does humor empower? What is the difference? When attempting to write this book and discuss the strength of humor, three things came to mind. There is humor <u>about</u> Appalachian people, humor that comes <u>from</u> Appalachia and there is humor directed <u>toward</u> the Appalachian lifestyle. For a "hillbilly" to tell a joke about hillbillies, you can expect they are probably having a good laugh at themselves. Enter the outsider. Should they crack off a joke about the redneck hillbilly, you can almost guarantee their humorous stories have met with successful laughter from peers. Every one of us has a painful memory of a time when we were the blunt of a joke or the patsy of a painful pun. Do you remember what you felt like when others laughed at your expense? There is a great difference between the humor of life experience and what you felt in that moment.

Humor <u>about</u> Appalachia and <u>from</u> Appalachia is a powerful resource that has made the mountain people strong over the years! That humor has kept a proud people smiling in the hardest of times. Humor from Appalachian writings and folktales has delivered to American culture many colorful metaphors, similes, idioms, slang and figurative language styles. They have been the tools of color and expression to the prose of our mountain authors. Humor directed toward our culture has challenged us to work through societies stereotyping.

Appalachian Humor

Mixed in with the humor of Appalachian writing, you will find many common themes in our folktales. You will find stories that speak to our need to understand and make sense of our existence; stories about the common person; trickster fables of fun and frolic; legends with supernatural elements; tales that validate certain aspects of culture, conformity, escape from the poverty and repressions of life; and stories of characters who overcame difficult situations, and rites of passage. Whether in folktale literature, a joke, or a story passed on by uncle Willie, Appalachian humor has always been a very powerful medicine. In it we find a release from stress and anger and a good sense of humor can help us better work through troubled times. We all need a good dose of laughter. One of my favorite Bible verses already mentioned says: "Laughter is as a good medicine". Can you remember how alive you felt after a good belly laugh? That good feeling can change our entire outlook on life's situations. If you look at the history of the Appalachian people, you will see that this medicine of humor was born of necessity into the hearts of a people who needed an escape from the harsh realities of their world.

> *"Laughter helps us see that the small things of life are not so earth shaking after all. It helps us look at a problem from a different point of view. It puts us in mind that our situation is not so traumatic after all."*

In regard to relationships, humor is said to bind us together, lighten our burdens and help us keep things in perspective. At our place of work, in our marriage and with our family, humor should be at the core. A good laugh can help us see the silver lining instead of clouds of storm. One of the major things that cause division in relationships today is that we have no release for all that high energy output used to simply cope with life's circumstances, problems and personal limitations. Laughter is that good medicine which binds us together and strengthens relationships! Laughter with our friends, neighbors and family can serve to lighten our load and create a bond that is hard to break. Laughs and smiles are enjoyed best when you give them away.

Humor from Appalachia comes in many forms and fashions. Humor from the Appalachian states has been called many things. The core is often loud, raw and yet often realistic about our way of life. Fiction and non-fiction pieces of literature from Appalachia have not gone unnoticed on the international scene. Literary giants in Boston and London's societies recognized Mark Twain, one of the most renowned frontier authors, for his wonderful descriptive writings characterizing backwoods characters from the South. William Faulkner was another popular writer who raised eyebrows in his time when it came to writing. His creative style makes him one of those who stand out among Southern humorist.

> *"Looking closely, you may notice that the comic relief of some authors often hits too close to home. For the reader, some have still yet to embrace their culture and the sometimes dark-side of the region."*

Choosing the profession of author, especially an author of humor, has not always been on the list of great occupations on the frontier and in the South. For those that chose this way of expression, success and acceptance was not always the case. Readers may sometimes be offended, naive to the truth or even have a hard time accepting what authors have written as "humor". To many of the Southern authors, both hard times and the lot in life of the Appalachian family have provided a wealth of colorful stories, tales, fables and fictional writing success (Inge 1975). **One thing to notice, however, is that humor from Appalachia is not written at the expense of others.** The focus of this chapter is not to throw a cold washcloth on the idea of humor, but we must challenge the idea that humor is not humorous when it is at the expense of any culture. This very issue was thrown into the national limelight in the spring of 2007. There is now a very popular radio host who is unemployed because he chose to make a tasteless attempt of humor at the expense of the African American culture. Point made!

If you study Southern humor writing, it fits into several periods of time. The writers during the years of 1830-1860 were "yarn-spinners" of comic proportions. Although not the intent of these authors, many stereotypes were sparked during this time. Those wild and crazy frontier characters paved the way for the modern day "redneck" image of sorts. Most of the authors of that period used pseudonyms to write. They included authors such as Augustus Longstreet, William Thompson, Thomas Thorpe, Johnson Hooper and George Harris. In that day, authors wanted to keep themselves separate from their characters to perhaps express some part of themselves that they undoubtedly could not express if others knew the real author.

From 1860 to 1925 a Western author who came to write about the South and tales from Appalachia came to prominence. That man was Mark Twain. He was considered by some to be one of the all time greatest literary comedians, and he was known for his colorful prose. Another popular and colorful writer of this era was Bill Arp. The writing style of Joel Harris and his Uncle Remus stories drew thousands of readers to Appalachian humor after the Civil War.

The golden age of Southern writing was 1925-1945. The greatest of the Southern authors made their mark on the literary world during this writing era. Writers like William Faulkner and Erskine Caldwell made humorous works of literature stand out with flair. There was not only a rise in humorous literature, but there was a new acceptance of American comedy in magazines, films and radio (Watkins, 1998).

Finally, from 1945 until now, there have been many high quality Southern humorists. To mention names like Flannery O'Connor, Eudora Welty, and Walker Percy would be to highlight some of the best. Other names come to mind of those who have impacted Southern literature such as William Price's "Fox's Southern Fried", Guy Owens's "The Ballad of the Flim-Flam Man", Mac Hyman's "No Time for Sergeants" and Loyal Jones' "Laughter in Appalachia" series. There are many other great authors of humor who lived, live and will live in Appalachia. I challenge you to pick up a book, sit back and enjoy the colorful prose of our greatest authors.

> *"Crossing the line from humorous writing to humor directed at any culture is a fine line that is hard to see and define. The challenge being made here is to examine when the 'humor' is more derogatory than humorous. The stereotypes promoted by many Southern writers and comedians are a perception and expression of our culture, but it is also how most of the world sees Appalachia."*

Humor directed at Appalachia

There is a genre of writing out there that does cross the line from good taste in humor to humor not in good taste. If you have had opportunity to read some of today's popular books, articles and comics, or listen to several popular stand-up comedians, there is a theme that permeates much of their work. The authors of such material call it humor. To most it is humorous, but to many it speaks of stereotyping and the promotion of an unrealistic image. There is plenty of ethnic and minority humor out there, but "hillbilly or redneck" humor seems to be highly popular right now. Bringing a specific image to the reader or to the public is why writers and humorists do what they do. It brings laughs and it makes money. The continued challenge from this author is that we be sensitive of that line between humor and humiliation.

What does stereotyping do for a rural population? It creates a generation of people who buy into a false truth about Appalachian life and embraces the stereotypical images portrayed. This is not a social problem isolated within the mountain culture, but a social problem none-the-less. This stereotypical imaging of Appalachia is no different than the injustice we see in the racial and ethnic profiling of African American or Middle East cultures now common in America. The stereotyping of the mountain culture has gone on for decades. And so for the Appalachian, like many other cultures, we live with the stereotypes placed upon us (Billings, 2001).

> *"If we hear something long enough, we begin to believe it. If we begin to believe it, our skewed view becomes the norm by which we perceive any culture of people."*

What is the social fall out of such humorous stereotyped imagery of the Appalachian people? It sets a person on a course to prove that the stereotype is either right or wrong. We often call it self-fulfilling prophesy. I remember moving to Kentucky and back to the roots of my family as a young man with my new wife and struggling in my early years as an "outsider" to the culture. One of the common questions I am still asked 24 years later is: "Are you from around here?" I always answer yes! Although I was a stand out with my

"Northern" accent and my misunderstanding of "the way things are done around here", I set out on a coarse to become part of my culture. I have learned to develop a sense of belonging to the region and it was a journey that met with success. It has been so successful that when I call my brother in Indiana, he makes fun of <u>my</u> accent. And yes, we both find a Northern/Southern banter humorous.

What does humor directed at Appalachia promote? One of the social trends of our day, regardless of where you live, is to place people into a mold based upon their religious, ethnic or cultural background. While visiting in Acuna, Mexico last spring on mission, one of the locals I met helped make my point. When I told him I was from Kentucky in the USA he asked me in broken English: "Why are you wearing shoes?" I have also heard some say: "It seems strange that an intelligent, educated person would actually move into a 'hick' town by choice". Where should we draw the line? You must answer that for yourself. The worn-out jokes about hillbillies and rednecks will probably persist as long as there are humorists. Most of us, as adults, have become immune to the imagery and even sometimes find a laugh or two at our own expense. But, what about our youth who have been born and raised here? Again, I ask that you find that line for yourself. My mission in this text is to get us to begin the dialog about humor found within a culture and humor that degrades a culture.

The truth be known, many of the youth I work with here in Kentucky have found that being stereotyped creates roadblocks to economic and educational success for them. It's not uncommon to hear someone say to a graduating senior: "If you want to make something of yourself, you have to move away". There's probably no better example of a self-fulfilling prophecy than that statement. Although the resources in Appalachia are minimal, it doesn't mean our culture is disadvantaged, poor, illiterate, low class, uneducated or unproductive (Billings, 2001).

> *"Breaking the status quo stereotype is the task at hand for all of us. We have to break the mindset of society and celebrate Appalachia. Appalachia is Ablaze with character, quality, joy and promise."*

Lest you finish this chapter with a bad taste in your mouth, I remind you that not all humor from Appalachia is stereotypical or in bad taste. If for some reason you are from the North and the pull of the highlands draws you to Appalachia, there are some things you need to know before you move here. Here is a quick education regarding our culture.

In urban America there are coffee houses, but when you move South you drink your coffee at the Waffle Houses. For breakfast, our friends from the North eat Cream of Wheat. In the South we eat grits. When I visit my childhood town in the North, I ask for a garden salad, but at home the waitress brings collard greens. The North has lobster, but in the South we eat crawdads. The North has the rust belt, but the South has the Bible belt.

The first Southern expression that creeps into a person's vocabulary when you move South is the adjective "big'ol". If you run your car into a ditch, don't worry too much. A "big'ol" boy in a "big'ol" four-wheel drive pickup truck with a tow chain will be along shortly. Don't worry about paying him or trying to help. Just sit back and watch. He lives for just that moment.

Don't be surprised to find movie rentals and bait in the same store. If you get stuck there for a while, feel free to use the tanning bed or get your nails done. They will probably have a grill too, but don't eat there. Remember, "y'all" is singular, plural, <u>and</u> plural possessive. Get used to hearing the question: "You ain't from around here, are you?" Let's go eat is abbreviated "Sqweet" in Appalachia. Don't be worried at not understanding what people are saying, because they can't understand you either. Get your camera ready for World's Funniest Videos and prepare for an interesting experience if you happen to hear someone holler: "Hey, y'all, watch this". If you do hear it, it would be wise to move out of the way. When you come up on anyone driving 15 mph down the middle of the road, remember that most of us have learned to drive on a John Deere. This is the proper speed and position for that vehicle. Most 10-year-olds own their own shotguns, and their moms are the ones who taught them how to shoot. If you do choose to settle in Appalachia and have children, don't think we will accept them as Appalachian. After all, if the cat had kittens in the oven, we wouldn't call them biscuits.

The healing power of laughter

The Healing Power of Humor is not a secret. One of the most powerful affects of laughter is its healing power. If you were to study the chemical reaction of the brain and body you would find that laughter activates a set of body chemicals. Those chemicals work to make a person's mental state of mind better to fight off illness and increase a person's will to live. For years, the Appalachian people have used humor as a healing balm. It has been their wellness factor. Healing humor is not the type of humor that batters their self-esteem. Healing humor is the type of humor that is positive, encouraging, friendly, joyous, and persuades people that you care about them rather than feel superior over them. The humor and colorful literature from Appalachia has brought out horrid truths that were hard to communicate in other ways. So they use humor. The healing power of Appalachian humor somehow makes a connection to the soul. It gives us hope to work harder, work together, and it releases an inner creativity that is hard to explain. It pulls our people together and lightens the burdens we carry (Moody, 1978).

The humor found in our region often focuses on life styles and events of the past. Often this humor is a way of healing through tragedy and trial. It doesn't attempt to change the past, but has been successful in changing tragedy's perspective. There have been times in my life where I have shed so many tears; I had no more to shed. Now I can laugh, because I've done all the crying I can do! The past is healed when we look at the bigger picture, drop our fears and see past tragedy and trial through a smile. Laughter sets the spirit free. Charlie Chaplain said: "To truly laugh, you must be able to take your pain and play with it." Laughing and crying can both be healing actions. Solomon of Bible fame wrote that there is a time to laugh, a time to cry and a season for everything under the sun. Humor relieves the mind, will and emotions of hurt, anxiety, stress, tension, fear, and the many negative emotions of life. Appalachian humor is a tool that delivers hope to future generations (Schaef, 1990). The bottom line is this:

"Humor is healing when its purpose is to bring joy and renewal to the soul. Humor is healing when it distracts us for a moment from the cares that burden us down. What you will find within Appalachia is the impact humor has upon our culture. Life's pressing emotions do not look so pressing through the eyes of laughter."

CHAPTER NINE

APPALACHIAN ALTRUISM, HOSPITALITY AND HUMILITY:

"Come On In"

Appalachia is a special place where hospitality reigns supreme. One of my favorite brushes with Southern hospitality was on a home visit for the church in my first years of ministry. I drove up to this quaint little home: complete with picket fence, pinwheel lawn decorations and an inviting front porch swing. When I knocked on the door, I heard a faint little voice say: "Come on in". Not accustomed to just walking into peoples homes, I knocked again. "I said, come on in honey!" As I opened the screen door and peered into the living room, there sat a sweet white haired lady. You would have thought I was a long lost relative. That afternoon I experienced true Southern hospitality. I tasted one of the best homemade apple pies of a lifetime, drank two cups of coffee, sat through a beginner's lesson on quilting, viewed the entire family album (dating back to the late 1800's) and perused her beloved flower garden.

I understand a little better now why grandma always wanted to feed us until we burst, and why she brought us a piece of cake, even when we had just left the table. I understand why she made dozens of jars of apple butter and gave them away. She always put up shelves of canned beans, beats and tomato juice, but gave most of it away. Her comment was: "I'm putting these away for hard times."

"The beauty of what my grandmother did was that she wasn't talking about hard times for herself and the family. She was talking about help and hospitality for others. She was talking about Southern Altruism."

How do you define real altruism? Altruism is lived in Appalachia not defined. However, to give it some meat, we will say altruism is: volunteering to help someone else, performing an intentional random act of kindness at a cost to you, with no intention of ever being repaid. I would be naive to believe Appalachia is the only place where altruism is strong, but I believe it is one of our strongest qualities (Miller, 1993). Southern highlanders seem to be highly aware of the needs of others and possess an inner drive to meet those needs. Why? I believe it is a lesson on social responsibility learned early in life. The term "social responsibility" basically refers to a person's feeling of obligation to help others even if they are unable to return the favor. If that altruistic behavior is reinforced positively, it will be repeated. This "Good Samaritan" mentality is one of our strongest themes in the mountains. It is this "Golden Rule" strongly taught in Appalachia which builds helping communities and helping homes (Grant, 2001).

"I feel strongly that many of our social perceptions, especially social responsibility, are taught through personal experience and learned behavior. If we see it modeled in our environment, we are more likely to be altruistic in nature."

One afternoon, on my way home from work, I ran out of gas. There was no one around, and I was stuck in the middle of nowhere. An older man stopped to help me. He pulled a gas can out of the back of his pickup truck and emptied it into my gas tank. As he got back into his truck to drive away, I asked if I could pay him for the gas and his time. His answer threw me. He said, "Son, you can repay me by stopping to help the next person you see along the side of the road. It may be my son or daughter." My experience may sound like a line from a popular movie, but it is an everyday experience in Appalachia. This is an example of Southern Altruism. When teaching on human behavior, I try to help those in the session see that it's not just important to walk a mile in another's moccasins. You need to know how their moccasins are made. Southern Altruism goes beyond helping those you see in need. It is about searching for those in need. It is almost a mission of altruism. Many exercise it through the church. Many exercise it through community action groups. Many exercise it through attaching themselves to altruistic clubs whose mission includes hospitality to the poor, sick and at-risk. One theory I have on factors hindering acts of kindness is that people just "don't take time to be kind". To be altruistic, a person must first have the heart and then make the time to help others. We take no time anymore to help others in need. One of the major factors that hinder us from reaching out to others is that we hit the ground running in the morning and don't stop until we lay our heads down at night. Secondly, we are often too afraid of taking the risk and becoming vulnerable to the world.

"In our hectic world, we have too much on our platter to factor in the intrusion of stopping to help others. It takes time to be kind, and most of us have a short supply of time."

Why are those in the South highly aware of the needs of others? I chalk it up to a personality of a people who are by character more laid back and relaxed. We stop and smell the roses. We take the time to look around at the needs of others. It is a strong bent toward altruistic behavior. I know we do not have the corner on caring, so for those in our society who are also bent toward altruistic behavior, God bless you. In Appalachia, if a friend or family member is in need...plan on the mountain being moved. The altruistic influences of the Judeo-Christian ethic and the kindly influence of multiple cultures are Ablaze in the Appalachian culture. These highly held value systems, altruistic norms and beliefs have influenced us, promote taking care of the stranger, the immigrant and the neighbor. It was custom in the Jewish culture to keep a light burning in the window as a welcome sign for traveling strangers who needed a safe harbor to rest. Although our society may not know the origins of the practice, it is very common to see candles adorning the windows of our homes. The Hebrew account of Elisha in the wilderness is a prime example of the altruistic attitude of giving. The prophet came upon a woman who had only enough flour and oil to make a last meal. After the meal, she had come to grips that she and her son would then perish from starvation. When the prophet approached and asked for food, the widow gave him her last morsels of food. In return, a marvelous miracle was performed to provide her and her son with more flour and oil than they could possibly use. In the book of Matthew, it is recorded that Christ had a conversation with his disciples about this very subject of altruism. He commended those who would show compassion and caring for the stranger. "When saw we you hungry and fed you, naked and clothed you, sick and took care of you, in prison and visited you?" And Jesus said, "When you have done it to the least of these, you have done it unto me." (Matthew 25:37).

> *"These words remind me of why I do what I do. Life as a social worker is a chosen path for altruism. It's not about the job. It's about the people, the poor and the needy. It is about feeding the hungry, clothing the naked, visiting the sick, rehabilitation of the criminal and giving of self to make a difference in this world. It is about investing your life in others!"*

Survival in the mountains depended upon a philosophy of caring for others. My father-in-law John shared many stories of his childhood and the great depression of 1941. Quite often there would be entire homeless families who would appear on the back porch of his house. Many of them came off the trains that ran by their home in the mountains. Grandma Greenhill always had a pot of brown beans, milk and cornbread to share with those in need. That is the altruistic spirit of Appalachia. Displaced workers and proud breadwinners found themselves searching desperately for work to feed their families. It wasn't charity they were looking for; it was work to feed their family. If you received hospitality from a neighbor, it was an unspoken norm for you to return the favor whenever it was possible (Brestin, 1993).

Mountain people take care of themselves, and they give from the heart. For those who are unable to care for themselves, there is family. For centuries, multiple families have lived together under the same roof for both physical and financial support. Today, it is not unusual for a social worker in Appalachia to find multiple families in any given home. It wouldn't be a high estimate to say close to 15% of the children in rural America live in multi-generational homes. In some cases, it is a grandparent taking care of a grandchild. Some dual family structures are the result of removal from the home for abuse or neglect. Many times in those cases the best choice of placement is with a grandparent or supportive relative. The rise of kinship care in our area is a welcome phenomenon because the numbers of foster care homes in our region are minimal. When children are removed from the home, it makes sense to place them with immediate family or relatives rather than processing them into the Foster Care system. It provides them with an already established support system.

Given the fact Appalachia is a region of poverty, many dual family homes find mutual support by living together. One family relative may stay home with the children, while the others work. Some are the result of single parents moving back home with their children, or children may live with relatives because of incarceration of a parent. For whatever reason, it is a social issue of great proportion (Grant, 2001). If you will look back to a previous chapter in the book, you will find that the family traditions of yesteryear have influenced this great sense of caring for the extended family. As goes the family, so goes Appalachia.

> *"What you will hear in Kentucky is: 'family is family'. The desire to take care of your 'kin' is as much a part of the altruistic approach to life as being a Good Samaritan or living the Golden Rule."*

One of the grandparents who volunteers in our Partners Assisting Learning in School project explained one day: "It makes me feel great to greet parents and visitors when they come into our school. I love the time I get to spend with the children. I get more out of working with them than they get out of being with me. I feel I'm really making a difference in my old age." What an example. That wonderful volunteer of the year didn't give her time for herself. She gave it for the joy that comes in giving. That's altruism. One of the biggest complaints I receive from educators is that: "We're teaching a generation of children who have no manners!" There is some truth to that, and it's not just regionalized to Appalachia. It is a trend among an entire nation of children. They have lost touch with altruism and social responsibility.

> *"Social responsibility is a large umbrella under which the way we treat others plays a high priority. When taught and modeled, altruism and a hospitable spirit are contagious."*

When others see positive behavior, it becomes the social norm within that micro system, mezzo system or macro system. It sets up a norm for altruism and reciprocity. It becomes internalized into a way of life. It becomes motivation for positive self-esteem and satisfaction in life. Nothing makes you feel better than to help others. It helps us see that life is not about external reward, but is somehow about that intrinsic reward that comes when we help others.

A humble spirit, a willing heart and caring soul are all a part of the Appalachian mindset. The next time you are driving through Appalachia, don't think twice when a man calls you honey, or someone puts a dime in the parking meter for you. Don't give it a thought if someone goes the extra mile to make you feel at home. If you're out visiting, expect to stay for a piece of apple pie. Take time to smell the roses and admire the blue grass that covers the countryside. The bottom line is this:

> *"Appalachian altruism, hospitality and humility are alive and well in the mountains. It is part of our culture and way of life. The next time you are in the southern highlands, Come On In. Breathe the fresh air and slow down a little. You'll want to take it all in...in Appalachia!"*

Conclusion

It's hard to conclude something that you feel you have just begun. When we began this look into culture, the goal was to share with you some historical and perhaps new and fresh insights into Appalachia. I hope you were able to see what I see every day. This book has been the celebration of a culture that loves life and lives it to the fullest. The reason for approaching this book from the viewpoint of a social worker was to raise your awareness of the social issues of my people in the Southern Highlands. My goal was to help you understand the battlefields on which we fight and the challenges we face for intervention. Within these pages is a history of social life in Appalachia. Our region is ripe for social change and needy for an influx of resources. Perhaps by reading this book, you may choose to be one of our valuable resources one day. Our role as change agent and broker is to meet the physical, emotional and social needs of the people. I invite you to join us in service.

You may have picked up this book out of curiosity for Appalachia or a textbook for knowledge. I hope your curiosity has been satisfied. I hope your awareness is keener. WE are a strong culture, perhaps forgotten in the social realm, but we are resilient! You have seen the goodness of fit in a people whose stereotyping will not hold us down. As you observe the way society views the Appalachian people, I hope you see us differently after reading this book. Will you rise above the stereotypical opinion? If you will, you will see that Appalachia is Ablaze with an inner strength that you have to experience for yourself. This writing has been a delving into a social environment Ablaze with multi-cultural diversity. The roots of our Appalachian history grow deep and strong. Although we only touched on a few of the cultures that made Appalachia what it is today, I believe the taste you were given will only increase and expand your view of who we are and where we came from.

The Appalachian people have carried their values and beliefs with them from the past into the present, and we will continue to be strong in our faith in the future. The pages of this book brought to light, not only our denominational histories, but the social dilemma's that come with "extreme" religious practice. Belief fashions our way of life and our way of life defines who we are. The life of each of us is built upon cornerstones of character and personality. The personality of the Appalachian people is rich with self-determination, independence and pride. These qualities may hold us to a path of consequence, yet they are foundational to the cornerstone of our personality.

"Laughter makes the heart merry". This was the theme I hoped to deliver. The Appalachian people are a culture whose humor and light heartedness has become a healing balm for hard times. Hard times come and go in our culture, yet the merry heart covers the harshness and reality of our life experience. When I feel down and discouraged, I simply look at the smiling faces of children and listen to their laughter as they play. When the world I live in looks bleak, I stop to remember "joy comes in the morning".

Finally, our best quality shines in the hearts of those whose lives are a little better because someone cared. Randomly, an act of kindness screams "altruism" and "hospitality"! I count it all joy to live in a region whose culture passes on this type of character with humility.

This book was about getting to know my people. Did you catch a glimpse? Do you have a vision? You must know them to empower them. To empower them you must love them. To love them you must reach out to them. When you have done all this, you have become an agent for social empowerment!

FOR THE CHILDREN! FOR THE KINGDOM!

DAVID R. MESSER, MSW, CSSW

BIBLIOGRAPHY AND SUGGESTED READINGS

Chapter One

A HALLMARK OF APPALACHIAN CULTURE:
The traditional value system as an expression of culture.

Billings, Dwight B. & Blee, Kathleen (2000). *The Road to Poverty: The Making of Wealth and Hardship in Appalachia.* New York: Cambridge University Press. (University of Kentucky Library)

Drake, Richard (2001). *A History of Appalachia.* Lexington: University Press of Kentucky. (University of Kentucky Library

Eller, Ronald D. (1982). *Miners, Millhands and Mountaineers: The Industrialization of the Appalachian South, 1880-1930.* Knoxville: University of Tennessee Press. (University of Kentucky Library)

Inscoe, John. (1989). *Mountain Masters, Slavery, and the Sectional Crisis in Western North Carolina.* Knoxville: University of Tennessee Press. (University of Kentucky Library)

Jones, Loyal (1994). *Appalachian Values.* Ashland, KY: Jesse Stuart Foundation. (University of Kentucky Library)

Jones, Loyal. (1988). *Laughter in Appalachia*: *A Festival of Southern Mountain Humor.* New York: Ivy Books. (University of Kentucky Library)

Jones, Virgil Carrington (1974). *The Hatfields and the McCoys.* Atlanta: Mocking Bird Books. (University of Kentucky Library)

NASW (1999). *Code of Ethics.* Revised from 1996. National Association of Social Workers. Retrieved on May 18, 2007 from:
http://www.naswdc.org/pubs/code/code.asp (Internet Source)

Webster, William (1977). *Webster's New World Dictionary*. William Collins and World Publishing Co., Inc. (Personal Library)

Chapter Two

THOSE POOR ILLITERATE HILLBILLIES:
Living above the stereotypes of society.

Billings, Dwight B. (2001). *Confronting Stereotypes: Back Talk from an American Region*. Lexington: University Press of Kentucky. (University of Kentucky Library)

Eller, Ronald D. (1982). *Miners, Millhands and Mountaineers: The Industrialization of the Appalachian South, 1880-1930*. Knoxville: University of Tennessee Press. (University of Kentucky Library)

Jones, Virgil Carrington (1974). *The Hatfields and the McCoys*. Atlanta: Mocking Bird Books. (University of Kentucky Library)

Rogers, Mary (1980). *The Pine Mountain Story, 1913-1980*. Pine Mountain, KY: Pine Mountain Settlement School. (University of Kentucky Library)

Spivak, John L. (1980). *The Devil's Brigade; the Story of the Hatfield-McCoy Feud*. New York: Brewer and Warren, Inc. (University of Kentucky Library)

Timeline of the Hatfield- McCoy Feud. Author Unknown. Retrieved on May 18, 2007 from: http://www.cob.montevallo.edu/McCoyCA/timeline.htm.

Waller, Altina L. (1988). *Feud, Hatfield, McCoys and Social Change in Appalachia, 1860- 1900*. Chapel Hill: University North Carolina Press. (University of Kentucky Library)

Chapter Three

THE ROOTS OF APPALACHIA:
The multi-cultural heritage that reflects the crayon box of a nation.

Awiakta, Marilou (1978). *Abiding Appalachia: Where Mountain and Atom Meet*. Memphis: St. Luke's Press. (University of Kentucky Library)

Burnett, John G. (1890). *The Trail of Tears: A Birthday Story of Private John G. Burnett, Captain Abraham McClellan's Company, 2ⁿᵈ Regiment, 2ⁿᵈ Brigade, Mounted Infantry, Cherokee Indian Removal, 1838-39*. Retrieved on May 18, 2007 from: www.cherokee.org (Internet Source)

Cherokee Timeline 1450-1838. (2007). Author Unknown. Golden Ink Publishing. Retrieved on May 18, 2007 from: www.powersource.com/nation/dates/html (Internet Source)

Foster, R.F. (1988). *Modern Ireland 1600-1972*. London: Allen Lane Press. (University of Kentucky Library)

Furer, Howard B. (1972). *The Scandinavians in America: A Chronology and Fact Book*. Dobbs Ferry, New York: Oceana Publications, Inc. (Berea College Library)

Furer, Howard B. (1973). *The Germans in America 1607-1970*. Dobbs Ferry, New York. Oceana Publications, Inc. (University of Kentucky Library)

Galicich, Anne (1989). *The German Americans*. New York: Chelsea House Publishers. (Lexington Public Library)

Gibbs, David with Newcombe, Jerry (2003). *One Nation under God*. Seminole, Florida: Christian Law Association. (Personal Library)

Golway, Terry and Coffey, Michael (Editor) (1997). *The Irish in America*. New York: Hyperion Publishing. (University of Kentucky Library)

Griffin, William D. (1998). *The Irish Americans*. New York: Hugh Lauter Levin Associates. (University of Kentucky Library)

Hatt, Christine (1999). *The Peoples of North America before Columbus*. Austin, Texas: Raintree-Steck-Vaughn. (Carmel Clay Public Library)

Hendricks, Graeff, Pastorius, Graeff (1688). *Protest against Slavery*. No originals available. Retrieved on May 18th, 2007 from: http://members.fortunecity.com/robertjshea/germusa/protest3.htm

Lindberg, John S. (1971). *The background of Swedish Emigration to the United States: an economic and sociological study in the dynamics of migration*. New York: J.S. Ozer. (University of Kentucky Library)

McGill, Allyson (1988). *The Swedish Americans*. New York: Chelsea House Publishers. (Lexington Public Library)

Mails, Thomas E. (1996). *The Cherokee People: The Story of the Cherokee from Earliest Origins to Contemporary Times*. New York, NY: Marlowe and Company. (University of Kentucky Library)

Mankiller, Wilma (1993). *Mankiller: a chief and her people*. New York: St. Martins Press. (University of Kentucky Library)

Miller, Kerby A. & Wagner, Paul (1994). *Out of Ireland: The Story of Irish Emigration to America*. Washington D.C.: Elliott and Clark Publishing. (University of Kentucky Library)

Mulligan, Elizabeth (Sunday, January 18, 1970). *Accounts of the Cherokee Trail of Tears with reference to Princess Atahki.* St. Louis Post-Dispatch. Retrieved on May 18th, 2007 from: http://www.yvwiiusdinvnohii.net/history/princes.html (Internet Resource)

National Historic Trail. *The Cherokee Trail of Tears 1838-1839.* (2007). Retrieved on May 18, 2007 from: http://www.rosecity.net/tears/trail/tearsnht.html

O Grada, Cormac (1995). *The Great Irish Famine.* Cambridge: New York: Cambridge University Press. (University of Kentucky Library)

Perdue, Theda & Green, Michael D. (1995). *The Cherokee Removal: A brief history with documents.* Boston: Bedford Books of St. Martin Press. (University of Kentucky Library)

Phillips, Michael (2000). *The Mayflower and Emigration to New England. An article by Michael Phillips.* Maritime History. Retrieved on May 18, 2007 from: http:/www.cronab. demon.co.uk/mf.htm (Internet Source)

Rabb, Theodore K. (1964). *The Thirty Years' War: problems of motive, extent, and effect.* Boston: Heath Publishing. (The University of Kentucky Library)

The Trail of Tears. (1999). Trail of Tears Association Home Web Page. Retrieved on May 18, 2007 from: www.nationaltota.org/the-story/ (Internet Source)

Taylor, Orris (1998). *Our English/Puritan Heritage: What Led To the Puritan Emigration of the 1630's? An Article by Orris Taylor.* Retrieved on May 18, 2007 from: http:/hometown. aol.com/ntgen/hrtg/engl.html (Internet Source)

A Timeline of Events and References Leading up to and through the founding of Jamestown. (2000). Author Unknown. The Association for the Preservation of Virginia Antiquities. Retrieved on May 18, 2007 from:
http://www.apva.org/history/timeline.html (Internet Source)

Chapter Four

RELIGION IN APPALACHIA:
A culture shaped by belief.

Baxter, Norman Allen (1957). *History of the Freewill Baptists: a study of New England separatism.* Rochester, NY: American Baptist Historical Society. (Asbury Theological Seminary Library)

Beale, David O. (2000). *The Mayflower Pilgrims: Roots of Puritan, Presbyterian, Congregationalist, and Baptist Heritage.* Greenville, S.C.; Belfast, Northern Ireland: Ambassador-Emerald, International. (Maysville Community College Library)

Behney, J. Bruce & Eller, Paul Himmel & Krueger, Kenneth (1979). *The History of the Evangelical United Brethren Church.* Nashville: Abington Press. (Lexington Theological Seminary Library)

Benton, Angelo Ames (1975). *Church Cyclopaedia: A Dictionary of Church Doctrine, History, Organization and Ritual, and Containing Original Articles on Special Topics.* Detroit, MI: Gale Group Publishing. (Indiana University Library)

Bushman, Richard Lyman (1989). *The Great Awakening: Documents of the Revival of Religion, 1740-1745.* Chapel Hill: University of North Carolina Press. (Southern Baptist Theological Seminary Library)

Boice, James Montgomery (1986). *Foundations of the Christian Faith: a comprehensive and readable theology.* Downers Grove, IL: Intervarsity Press. (Kentucky Christian University Library)

Bowman, Carl & Bowman Carl F. & Kraybill, Donald B. (2001). *On the Backroad to Heaven: Old Order Hutterites, Mennonites, Amish, and Brethren.* Baltimore: Johns Hopkins University Press. (Lexington Theological Seminary Library)

Bowman, Carl F. (1995). *Brethren Society: The Cultural Transformation of a "Peculiar People."* Baltimore: The Johns Hopkins University Press.

Bowman, Loren S. (1987). *Power and Polity Among the Brethren: A Study of Church Governance.* Elgin, Illinois: Brethren Press.

Brackney, William H. (1999). *Historical dictionary of the Baptists.* Lanham, MD: Scarecrow Press. (University of Kentucky Library)

Collinge, William J. (1997). *Historical Dictionary of Catholicism.* Lanham, Maryland: Scarecrow Press. (Lexington Theological Seminary Library)

Cooper, Wilmer A. (1990). *A Living Faith: An Historical and Comparative Study of Quaker Beliefs.* Richmond, IN: Friends United Press. (Asbury Theological Seminary Library)

Dorgan, Howard (1990). *Giving Glory to God in Appalachia: Worship Practices of Six Baptist Sub-denominations.* Knoxville: University of Tennessee Press. (University of Kentucky Library)

ELCA—Evangelical Lutheran Church in America (2002) American *Lutheran Developments in Their Historical Context: Some Major Landmarks.* Prepared by the Evangelical Lutheran Church in America. (University of Kentucky Library, Internet Resource: www.elca.org)

Foster, Douglas; Blowers, Paul M.; Dunnavant, Anthony L.; Williams, D. Newell (2004). *The Encyclopedia of the Stone-Campbell Movement*. Grand Rapids, MI, Cambridge, UK: William B Eerdmans Publishing Company. (Kentucky Christian University Library)

Francis, Richard (2001). *Ann the Word: The Story of Ann Lee, Female Messiah, Mother of the Shakers, the Woman Clothed with the Sun*. New York: Arcade Publishing. (Morehead State University Library)

Frank, Isnard Wilhelm (1995). *A Concise History of the Mediaeval Church*. New York: Continuum Publishing. (Asbury Theological Seminary Library)

Gill, Frederick C. (1964). *Charles Wesley: the first Methodist*. London: Lutterworth Press. (University of Kentucky Library)

Gillett, E. H. & Gillett, Exera H. (2001). *Life and Times of John Huss: The Bohemian Reformation of the 15th Century*. New York: AMS Press. (Eastern Kentucky University Library)

Gordon, Bruce (2002). *The Swiss Reformation*. Manchester, UK: New York: Manchester University Press. (Asbury Theological Seminary Library)

Holmes, Urban T. (1982). *What is Anglicanism?* Wilton, Connecticut: Morehouse Barlow Co. (Asbury Theological Seminary Library)

Hostetler, John Andrew (1993). *The Amish Society*. Baltimore: Johns Hopkins University Press. (University of Kentucky Library)

Hostetler, John Andrew (1980). *Amish Children: Education in the Family, School, and Community*. Fort Worth, TX: Harcourt Brace Jovanovich. Second edition.

Hulse, Erroll (2001). *Who are the Puritans, and What Do They Teach?* Faverdale North, Darlington UK: Evangelical Press. (Morehead State University Library)

Hostetler, John Andrew (1989). *Amish Roots: A Treasury of History, Wisdom, and Lore*. Baltimore: Johns Hopkins University Press. (Boyd County Public Library)

Loewen, Eden K. & Loewen, Royden K. (1993). *Family, Church, and Market: A Mennonite Community in the Old and the New Worlds, 1850-1930*. Toronto: University of Toronto Press. (University of Kentucky Library)

Lutz, Charles P. (1985). *Church Roots: Stories of Nine Immigrant Groups That Became the American Lutheran Church*. Minneapolis: Augsburg Fortress Press. (Indianapolis-Marion County Public Library)

McBeth, H. Leon (1990). *A Sourcebook for Baptist Heritage* Nashville, TN: Broadman Press. (Southern Baptist Theological Seminary Library)

McBeth, H. Leon (1987). *The Baptist Heritage/Four Centuries of Baptist Witness*. Nashville, TN: Broadman Press. (Southern Baptist Theological Seminary Library)

McEllhenney, John G. & Maser, Frederick & Rowe, Kenneth E. & Yrigoyen, Charles (1992). *United Methodism in America: A Compact History*. Nashville, TN: Abingdon. (Southern Baptist Theological Seminary Library)

Mead, Frank S., Hill, Samuel S. (2001). *Handbook of Denominations in the United States*. Nashville, TN. Abingdon Press. (Kentucky Christian University Library)

Moorman, J. R. H. (1983). *The Anglican Spiritual Tradition*. Springfield, IL: Templegate Press. (University of Kentucky Library)

Nichols, Aidan (1992). *The Panther and the Hind: A Theological History of Anglicanism*. Edinburgh: T and T Clark Publishing. (Southern Baptist Theological Seminary Library)

Packer, J. I. (1990). *A Quest for Godliness: The Puritan Vision of the Christian Life*. Wheaton, IL: Crossway Books. (Asbury Theological Seminary Library)

Prichard, Robert (1991). *A History of the Episcopal Church*. Harrisburg, PA: Morehouse Publishing. (Lexington Theological Seminary)

Robertson, Edwin (1984). *John Wycliffe: morning star of the Reformation*. Basington: Marshal Press. (Southern Baptist Theological Seminary)

Russell, C. Allyn. (1976). *Voices of American Fundamentalism: Seven Biographical Studies*. Philadelphia: Westminster Press. (Morehead State University Library)

Selleck, Linda B. (1995). *Gentle Invaders: Quaker Women Educators and Racial Issues During the Civil War and Reconstruction*. Richmond, IN: Friends United Press. (Indiana University-Purdue University Indianapolis)

Stein, Stephen J. (1992). *The Shaker Experience: A History of the United Society of Believers, Called Shakers*. New Haven: Yale University Press. (University of Kentucky Library)

Smith, Frank Joseph (1985). *The History of the Presbyterian Church in America*. Manassas, VA: Reformation Education Foundation. (Louisville Presbyterian Theological Seminary Library)

Trevor-Roper, H. R. (1984). *Religion, the Reformation and Social Change, and other essays*. London: Secker and Warburg. (University of Kentucky Library)

Webber, Frank T. (1999). *Welcome to the Episcopal Church: An Introduction to Its History, Faith and Worship*. Harrisburg, PA: Morehouse Publishing. (Louisville Presbyterian Theological Seminary Library)

Wells, David F. and Nicole, Roger R. (1985). *Reformed Theology in America: a history of its modern development.* Grand Rapids, MI: W.B. Eerdmans Publishing Company. (Louisville Theological Seminary Library)

Young, B.W. (1998). *Religion and Enlightenment in Eighteenth-Century England: Theological Debate from Locke to Burke.* Oxford: Clarendon Press; New York: Oxford University Press. (University of Kentucky Library)

Yrigoyen, Charles Jr. & Warrick, Susan E. (1996). *Historical dictionary of Methodism.* Lanham, Md.: Scarecrow Press. (Louisville Presbyterian Theological Seminary Library)

Chapter Five

RELIGION AND SOCIAL DILEMMA:
Extreme beliefs that create social quandary.

Ankerberg, John & Weldon, John (1998). *Knowing the Truth About Eternal Security (Defenders Series).* Eugene, Oregon: Harvest House Publishers, Inc. (Personal Library)

Bettenson, Henry S. & Maunder, Chris (1999). *Documents of the Christian Church.* New York: Oxford University Press. (University of Kentucky Library)

Byrne, Peter, Houlden, Leslie (1995). *Companion Encyclopedia of Theology.* London; New York: Routledge Publishing. (Lexington Theological Seminary)

Corner, Daniel D. (2000). *The Believer's Conditional Security: Eternal Security Refuted.* Washington, PA: Evangelical Outreach. (Personal Library)

Fisk, Samuel (2002). *Election and Predestination: Keys to a Clearer Understanding.* Eugene, Oregon: Wipf and Stock Publishers. (Personal Library)

Horton, Michael Scott and Pinson, J. Matthew (2002). *Four Views on Eternal Security.* Grand Rapids, MI: Zondervan Publishing House. (Kentucky Christian University)

Melton, J. Gordon (1994). *The Encyclopedia of American Religions: Religious Creeds.* Detroit: Gale Research Inc. (University of Kentucky Library)

Richardson, Alan, & Bowden, John S. (1983). *A Dictionary of Christian Theology.* Philadelphia: Westminster Press. (University of Kentucky Library)

Routley, Erik (1963). *Creeds and confessions: from the reformation to the modern church.* Philadelphia: Westminster Press. (University of Kentucky Library)

Schreiner, Thomas R & War, Bruce A. (2000). *Still Sovereign: Contemporary Perspectives on Election, Foreknowledge, and Grace.* Grand Rapids, MI: Baker Book House. (Kentucky Christian University Library)

Stanley, Charles F. (1990). *Eternal Security: can you be sure?* Nashville: Thomas Nelson Press. (Lexington Public Library)

Swindoll, Charles R. (1993). *Eternal Security: The Assurance of Our Destiny.* Grand Rapids, MI: Zondervan Publishing House. (Personal Library)

Chapter Six

EXPRESSIONS OF THE APPALACHIAN CULTURE:
The roots of Appalachian music, art and craft

Allen, H. L. (1970). *American and European hand weaving Revised.* Madison, Wisconsin: College Printing.

Atkins, Jacqueline Marx (1994). *Shared Threads: Quilting Together, Past and Present.* New York: Viking Studio Books. (Morehead State University Library)

Awonitzer, Mark & Hirshberg, Charles (Contributor) (2002). *Will You Miss Me When I'm Gone? The Carter Family and Their Legacy in American Music.* New York: Simon & Schuster. (Morehead State University Library)

Breathnach, Breandan (1977). *Folk Music and Dances of Ireland.* Dublin: Mercier Ltd. (Indianapolis-Marion County Public Library)

Burch, Monte (2004). *Making Native American Hunting, Fighting and survival tools.* Guilford, Connecticut: Lyons Press. (Indianapolis-Marion County Public Library)

Cantwell, Robert. (1992). *Bluegrass Breakdown: The Making of the Old Southern Sound.* New York: DaCapo Press. (University of Kentucky Library)

Christensen, Erwin (1952). *Early American Woodcarving.* Cleveland: World Publishing Co. (University of Kentucky Library)

Conway, Cecelia (1995). *African Banjo Echoes in Appalachia: A Study of Folk traditions.* Knoxville: University of Tennessee Press. (University of Kentucky Library)

Dane, Suzanne G. & Sturni, Barbara E. (1990). *Feather Beds and Flapjacks.* Washington, D.C.: National Trust for Historic Preservation. (Lexington Public Library)

Epstein, Dena J. Polacheck (1981). *Sinful Tunes and Spirituals: Black Folk Music to the Civil War.* Urbana: University of Illinois Press. (University of Kentucky Library)

Ferrero, Pat, & Hedges, Elaine & Silber, Julie (1987). *Hearts and Hands: The Influences of Women and Quilts on American Society*. San Francisco: Quilt Digest Press. (University of Kentucky Library)

Goodrich, Frances L. & Goodrich, Francis Louisa (1989). *Mountain Homespun: a facsimile of the original*. Knoxville: University of Tennessee Press. (University of Kentucky Library)

Guilland, Harold F. (1971). *Early American Folk Pottery*. Philadelphia: Chilton Book Company. (University of Kentucky Library)

Hodges, Henry W. M. (1964). *Artifacts: an introduction to primitive technology*. New York: F.A. Praeger. (Morehead State University Library)

Irwin, John Rice (1982). *Baskets and basket makers in Southern Appalachia*. Exton, PA: Schiffer Publishing, Ltd. (University of Kentucky Library)

Kinsbury, Paul & Parton, Dolly (Introduction) (1995) *The Grand Ole Opry History of Country Music: 70 Years of the Songs, the Stars, and the Stories*. New York: Villard Books. (Eastern Kentucky University Library)

Olney, Warren (2002). *Early American Brooms: The art of making brooms*. Warren Olney Website: BroomShop.com (Internet Source)

Spalding, Susan Eike and Woodside, Jane Harris (1995). *Communities In Motion: dance, community, and tradition in America's Southeast and beyond*. Westport, Connecticut: Greenwood Press. (University of Kentucky Library)

Smith, Richard D. (2000). *Can't You Hear Me Callin': The Life of Bill Monroe, Father of Bluegrass*. Boston: Little Brown and Company. (Morehead State University)

Tolman, Beth and Page, Ralph (1976). *The Country Dance Book: the best of the early contras and squares, their history, lore, callers, tunes and joyful instructions*. Brattleboro, VT: S. Greene Press. (Eastern Kentucky University Library)

Wigginton, Eliot (1984). *Foxfire Eight: Southern folk pottery from pug mills, ash glazes, and groundhog kilns, face jugs, churns and roosters, mule swapping, chicken fighting...* Garden City, NY: Anchor Press/Doubleday. (University of Kentucky Library)

Wolfe, Charles K. (1997). *The Devil's Box: Masters of Southern Fiddling*. Nashville: Country Music Foundation Press and Vanderbilt University Press. (University of Kentucky Library)

Chapter Seven

SELF-DETERMINATION, INDEPENDENCE, AND PRIDE:
The cornerstones of social life in Appalachian culture.

Billings, Dwight B. & Blee, Kathleen (2000). *The Road to Poverty: The Making of Wealth and Hardship in Appalachia.* New York: Cambridge University Press. (University of Kentucky Library)

Deci, Edward L., & Ryan, R. M. (1985). *Intrinsic motivation and self-determination in human behavior.* New York: Plenum. (University of Kentucky Library)

Fisher, Stephen. (1993). *Fighting Back in Appalachia: Traditions of Resistance and Change.* Philadelphia: Temple University Press. (University of Kentucky Library)

Gaventa, John & Smith, Barbara & Willingham, Alex. (1990*). Communities in Economic Crisis: Appalachia and the South.* Philadelphia: Temple University Press. (University of Kentucky Library)

Haynes, Ada F. (1997). *Poverty in Central Appalachia: Underdevelopment and Exploitation.* New York: Garland Publishing. (University of Kentucky Library)

Chapter Eight

APPALACHIAN HUMOR OR HUMOR ABOUT APPALACHIA:
A look at humors impact upon a culture.

Billings, Dwight B. & Norman, Gurney & Ledford, Katherine (2001). *Confronting Stereotypes: Back Talk from Appalachia.* Lexington: University Press of Kentucky. (University of Kentucky Library)

Inge, M. Thomas (1975). *The Frontier Humorists: critical views.* Hamden, Connecticut: Archon Books. (University of Kentucky Library)

Jones, Loyal. (1987). *Laughter In Appalachia: A Festival of Southern Mountain Humor.* Little Rock: August House Publishing. (University of Kentucky Library)

Jones, Loyal (1995). *More Laughter In Appalachia: Southern Mountain Humor.* Little Rock: August House Publishing. (University of Kentucky Library)

Moody, Raymond A. (1978). *Laugh after Laugh: the healing power of humor.* Jacksonville, Florida: Headwaters Press. (University of Kentucky Library)

Schaef, Anne Wilson (1990). *Laugh! I Thought I'd Die (If I Didn't)* New York: Ballantine Books, Inc. (Indianapolis-Marion County Public Library)

Watkins, James (1998*). Southern Selves: From Mark Twain and Eudora Welty to Maya Angelou and Kaye Gibbons: A Collection of Autobiographical Writing.* New York: Vintage Books. (Indianapolis-Marion County Public Library)

Chapter Nine

APPALACHIAN ALTRUISM, HOSPITALITY AND HUMILITY:
"Come on in".

Blum, Lawrence A. (1980). *Friendship, altruism and Morality.* London; Boston: Routledge and K. Paul. (The University of Kentucky Library)

Brestin, Dee (1993). *The Joy of Hospitality: Recovering a Lost Art.* Chariot Victor Publishing. (Southern Baptist Theological Seminary)

Grant, Colin (2001). *Altruism and Christian Ethics.* Cambridge: Cambridge University Press. (Personal library. The book can be found at Cambridge University Library)

Margolis, Howard (1982*). Selfishness, Altruism, and Rationality: A Theory of Social Choice.* Cambridge; New York: Cambridge University Press. (The University of Kentucky Library)

Miller, Fred & Paul, Ellen & Paul Jeffrey (1993). *Altruism.* Cambridge: New York. Cambridge University Press. (Indiana University and Purdue University Indianapolis)

Monroe, Kristen R. (1996). *The Heart of Altruism: Perceptions of a Common Humanity.* Princeton, NJ: Princeton University Press. (The University of Kentucky Library)

Stark, Oded (1995). *Altruism and beyond: An Economic Analysis of Transfers and Exchanges within Families and Groups.* Cambridge; New York: Cambridge University Press. (The University of Kentucky Library)

Appendix A

TIMELINES OF OUR APPALACHIAN ANCESTORS

Timeline for the Hatfield and McCoy Conflict

1865   The first death in the feud was Asa Harmon McCoy. There was no prosecution. The Civil War ends in May.

1878   Randolph McCoy accuses Floyd Hatfield of stealing his pig.

1880   Bill Staton was murdered by Paris and Sam McCoy in June. Sam McCoy was tried in court for the death of Staton. He was acquitted. Roseanna McCoy and Johnse Hatfield agree to live together and live at Hatfield cabin.

1881   Roseanna returns home, then moves to aunt's cabin where McCoy boys capture Johnse. Roseanna's ride to Devil Anse's saves Johnse's life. Pregnant Roseanna returns to Ole Ran'l's home, catches measles, miscarries baby, and then moves to Pikeville. Johnse marries Nancy McCoy on May 14.

1882   Ellison Hatfield was fatally wounded by Bud, Tolbert and Pharmer McCoy. After his death on August 9, the three brothers are tied up and executed. During this year, Jeff McCoy is also killed on the banks of the Tug Fork.

1887   The Kentucky governor appoints Frank Phillips to capture the McCoy boys' murderers.

1888   The Hatfields New Year's Day raid on Randle McCoy's cabin leaves Alifair and Calvin McCoy dead and their home burned to ground. Roseanna McCoy, less than 30 years old, dies in Pikeville.

1889   The trial of the Hatfield clan for the McCoy murders begins.

1890   Ellison Mounts was executed for Alifair McCoy's murder.

1891   The Hatfield and McCoy Feud ends.

Information retrieved on May 18, 2007 from:

http://www.cob.montevallo.edu/McCoyCA/timeline.htm

Appendix B

TIMELINES OF OUR APPALACHIAN ANCESTORS

A Timeline of the Cherokee Nation

1540   The Cherokees in their homeland are discovered by the Spanish explorer Hernando DeSoto and his party.

1673   The first traders from English settlements begin trading among the Cherokees.

1721   The Charleston Treaty with the Governor of the Carolinas is thought to be the first concession of Cherokee land.

1785   The Treaty of Hopewell is the first treaty between the United States and the Cherokee.

1791   The Treaty of Holston is signed, which called for the U.S. government to advance a "civilization" of Cherokees by giving them farm tools and technical advice.

1802   Thomas Jefferson signs the Georgia Compact in support of Indian removal.

1817   Cherokee lands are exchanged for land in Arkansas by the signing of a treaty.

1821   The Sequoyah's Cherokee syllabrey was completed and helped to increase the literacy level of the Cherokees.

1822   The Cherokee Supreme Court was established.

1825   New Echota, Georgia was established as the Cherokee capital.

1827   An early "modern" Cherokee Nation began with a Cherokee Constitution was established at a convention, where John Ross was elected chief.

1828   The Cherokee Phoenix (the first Native American and bilingual newspaper written in Cherokee and English) was published. Gold was discovered on Cherokee land in Georgia.

1828-30 The Georgia Legislature "abolished" the tribal government of the Cherokee and then took control over their lands.

1832   Our U.S. Supreme Court's decision in the Worcester vs. Georgia case established tribal sovereignty. It protected the Cherokees from Georgia laws. President Jackson refused to enforce the U.S. Supreme Court decision and Georgia held a lottery for Cherokee lands.

1835   A small minority of 100 Cherokees signed the Treaty of New Echota giving the title to all Cherokee lands in the Southeast to the United States in exchange for land in Indian Territory. The signers and their supporters are thereafter referred to as members of the Treaty Party.

1838   U.S. government forces removed 17,000 Cherokees to Indian Territory in defiance of the U.S. Supreme Court decision. More than 4,000 die from exposure and disease on the trip.

1839   Treaty Party leaders Major Ridge, John Ridge and Elias Boundinot are assassinated for signing the Treaty of New Echota. A new constitution was ratified at a convention in Tahlequah, which unites Cherokees arriving from the east and the west.

1860   Tension mounts between the Union Cherokees and Confederate sympathizers. Chief Ross strives to keep the Cherokee Nation neutral.

1861   Chief Ross was forced to side with the Confederacy after Union troops abandon Indian Territory. The Cherokee Nation was torn by warfare that took place along their lands.

1889   Unassigned lands in Indian Territory are opened to white settlers known as "boomers."

1893   The Cherokee Outlet was opened for settlement by whites. The Dawes Commission arrived to begin taking a census or roll of the Cherokee.

1903   William C. Rogers becomes the last elected Cherokee chief for 68 years.

1905   A land allotment begins after the "official" Dawes Commission Roll was taken of the Cherokee nation.

1917   Chief William C. Rogers dies.

1934   The Indian Reorganization Act establishes a land base for tribes and a legal structure for self- government.

1948   A Cherokee Convention was called which lays the ground for a modern Cherokee Government.

1949   W.W. Keeler is appointed as the Cherokee chief by President Harry Truman.

1961   The Cherokee are awarded $15 million by the U.S. Claims Commission for Cherokee Outlet lands.

1970   U.S. Supreme Court ruling confirms Cherokee, Choctaw and Chickasaw Nation's ownership of 96-mile segment of Arkansas Riverbed.

1971   W.W. Keeler becomes first elected principal chief since statehood.

1975   Ross O. Swimmer is elected to the first of three terms as principal chief

1976   Cherokee voters ratify a new "modern" Cherokee Constitution.

1985   Wilma Mankiller fulfills the remainder of Ross O. Swimmer's term as principal chief.

1987   Chief Mankiller becomes the first woman elected principal chief.

1988   The Cherokee Nation and the Eastern Band of Cherokees gather in Cherokee, N.C. to commemorate the Trail of Tears.

Information retrieved on May 18th, 2007 from:

www.powersource.com/nation/dates/html

Appendix C

TIMELINES OF OUR APPALACHIAN ANCESTORS

A Timeline of English Americans And Important Dates

1558   Queen Elizabeth succeeds Queen Mary.

1562   Jean Ribault established the Huguenot colony called Fort Charles at Port Royal in South Carolina. An explorer named John Hawkins made his first voyage to the West Indies.

1563   Fort Charles was abandoned.

1564   A second colony of Huguenots was started on the St. John's River in Florida. John Hawkins also made a second voyage to the West Indies and Guinea.

1567   John Hawkins third voyage took place.

1568   Hawkins was caught in skirmishes with the Spanish and engages in what historians call the Battle of Vera Cruz.

1578   England enters into a treaty with the Netherlands to fight against Spain.

1580   Sir Francis Drake comes back to England from his "around the world" voyage.

1585   Raleigh's fleet of seven vessels reaches Roanoke Island in June.

1586   In June, Sir Francis Drake arrives from Florida and removes the Lane colony to England.

1587   John White was sent by Sir Walter Raleigh to plant the City of Raleigh on the Chesapeake Bay.

1602   Sir Walter Raleigh sent Samuel Mace on a voyage to Virginia (North Carolina). The goal of the trip was to gather plant materials and to search for survivors of the Lost Colony. Back in Scotland, James VI becomes James I.

1608   Newport returns to Jamestown with the first supplies and about 100 new settlers. He finds only 38 survivors and that the town had been burnt. New settlers began to rebuild the town and build new forts for protection. Newport brings back a second supply ship along with Dutch and Polish settlers.

1610   Sr. Thomas Gates was serving as Virginia's first governor. He issues the Divine, Moral, and Martial Law in and around Jamestown. He later decides to abandon Jamestown.

1611   John Rolfe imports tobacco seeds from Trinidad to compete with the native tobacco.

1612   John Rolfe exports the first crop of improved tobacco.

1613   Pocahontas is captured and brought to Jamestown.
1614   John Rolfe and Pocahontas get married at Jamestown.
1616   John Rolfe, Pocahontas, and their son depart Virginia for England.

Information retrieved on May 18, 2007 from:

http://www.apva.org/history/timeline.html

Appendix D

TIMELINES OF OUR APPALACHIAN ANCESTORS

A Timeline of the Irish in Early America

1492   Christopher Columbus sails to the New World. William Eris (or Ayers), an Irishman from Galway, is reportedly amongst the crew. He is said to be one of the forty volunteers left behind in Hispaniola and said to be killed by indians after Columbus' departure.

1598   An Irish rebellion against the English began.

1600   The most determined resistance to England came from Ulster (the northeastern part of the island). In putting down the rebellion, English forces tore up the Ulster countryside. Once these chieftains had submitted, King James I of England was willing to let them live on their ancestral lands as English-style nobles. Dissatisfied with their token roles, the chieftains headed for America in 1607.

1644   Daniel Gookin (1612-1687), son of an early Irish settler in Virginia, moves to Massachusetts and eventually becomes a member of the Governor's Council, major general of the militia, and superintendent of Indian affairs.

1649   Oliver Cromwell quickly imposed English authority on Ireland. Cromwell repaid his soldiers and investors in the war effort with land confiscated largely from the Anglo-Irish Catholics of the Irish.

1652   A list of inhabitants of Dublin was collected.

1652   Thousands of Irish men and women were involuntarily "transported" as laborers to the West Indies by Cromwell's forces. Many of these people and their descendents later moved to the United States.

1776   Men of Irish birth or descent formed between one-third to one-half of the American Revolutionary forces, including 1,492 officers and 26 generals.

1776   Boston was evacuated by British troops on March 17, and General Washington assigned "St. Patrick" the password of the day. The Declaration of Independence was signed in Philadelphia in July.

1777   Irish and Irish-Americans were said to have represented between one-third and one-half of the Revolutionary forces, including almost 1500 officers and 26 generals.

1779   The first St. Patrick's Day parade took place in New York City.

1790   The first census of the United States records 44,000 Irish-born residents, half of which lived south of Pennsylvania.

1791   Irishman James Hoban designs the White House. It was copied after the Leinster House in Dublin, Ireland.

1798   Many distinguished survivors of the failed revolutionary uprising of the Society of United Irishmen, including President William McKinley's grandfather, began arriving in the United States.

1814   The Irish Emigrant Society was founded in New York City to meet new arrivals from Ireland, protect them from being exploited by swindlers and boardinghouse keepers, and aid them in establishing themselves in America.

1829   The Emancipation Act in England lifts penalties for Irish Catholics and Presbyterians.

1830   Over the next 10 years, 237,000 Irish immigrants entered the United States.

1840   Until the year 1850, the Great Famine strikes, more than 1,000,000 Irish men and women emigrate.

1840   800,000 Irish immigrants enter the United States over the course of the next 10 years.

Information retrieved on May 18, 2007 from:

http://memory.loc.gov/ammem/ndlpedu/features/immig/irish2.html

Appendix E

TIMELINES OF OUR APPALACHIAN ANCESTORS

A German Timeline in Early America

1608   Several Germans were among the settlers at Jamestown.

1626   Peter Minuit, a German, came to New Amsterdam to serve as the governor of the Dutch colony, New Netherlands. Later he governed the Swedish colony in Delaware.

1683   Thirteen German Mennonite families who sought religious freedom arrived in Pennsylvania. Led by Franz Pastorius, they purchased 43,000 acres of land and founded Germantown six miles north of Philadelphia.

1700s   The settling of the British colonies by small German-speaking religious groups continued. The groups included Swiss Mennonites, Baptist Dunkers, Schwenkfelders, Moravians, Amish, and Waldensians; most German immigrants belonged to the main Lutheran and Reformed churches. German settlers designed and built the Connestoga wagon, which was used in the opening of the American Frontier.

1731   Protestants were expelled from Salzburg, Austria, in this year. They subsequently founded Ebenezer, Georgia.

1732   The first German-language newspaper, *Philadeophische Seitung*, was published in the United States. German publishing flourished in Philadelphia and in smaller communities such as Ephrata, Pennsylvania.

1733   John Peter Zenger, who came to America as an indentured servant from the Palatinate region of Germany, founded *The New-York Weekly Journal*.

1741   Moravians founded Bethlehem and Nazareth, Pennsylvania.

1742   Christopher Saur, a German printer in Philadelphia, printed the first Bible in America.

1778   General Friedrich Wilhelm von Steuben, a Prussian officer, became inspector general of the Continental Army.

1783   As many as 5,000 of the Hessian soldiers hired by Britain to fight in the Revolutionary War remained in America after the end of hostilities.

1790   By this date as many as 100,000 Germans may have immigrated to America.

1821   Pennsylvania Dutch in Lancaster, Pennsylvania introduced the Germanic custom of having a specially decorated tree at Christmas time to America. Later in the century they introduced St. Nicholas who evolved into America's Santa Claus. German immigrants also brought the Easter bunny and Easter eggs to this country.

1836   John Nepomucene Neumann arrived in the United and founded the first American diocesan school system. In 1977 Pope Paul VI canonized him as a saint.

1847   The Missouri Synod of the Lutheran Church was founded by German immigrants to combat what they saw as the liberalization of Lutheranism in America.

1850s   Nearly one million Germans immigrated to America in this decade, one of the peak periods of German immigration; in 1854 alone, 215,000 Germans arrived in this country.

1860   An estimated 1.3 million German-born immigrants resided in the United States

1880s   In this decade, the decade of heaviest German immigration, nearly 1.5 million Germans left their country to settle in the United States; about 250,000, the greatest number ever, arrived in 1882.

1890   An estimated 2.8 million German-born immigrants lived in the United States. Majorities of the German-born living in the United States were located in the German triangle, whose three points were Cincinnati, Milwaukee, and St. Louis.

1933   The coming to power of Adolf Hitler in Germany caused a significant immigration of leading German scientists, writers, musicians, scholars, and other artists and intellectuals to the United States to escape persecution. Among them were such notables as Albert Einstein. By the end of World War II, there were some 130,000 of these German and Austrian refugees living in America.

1950s   Between 1951 and 1960, 580,000 Germans immigrated to the United States.

1960s   Between 1961 and 1970, 210,000 Germans immigrated to the United States.

1970s   Between 1971 and 1980, 65,000 Germans immigrated to the United States.

1983   The United States and Germany celebrated the German-American Tricentennial, marking the 300th anniversary of German immigration to Pennsylvania.

1987   German-American Day was established by Congressional resolution and presidential proclamation.

1990   According to the Bureau of the Census, 58 million Americans claimed to be solely or partially of German descent.

Information retrieved on May 18, 2007 from:

http://oriole.umd.edu/~mddlmddl/791/communities/html/germanic.html

http://oriole.umd.edu/~mddlmddl/791/communities/html/germania.html

Made in the USA
Thornton, CO
03/14/23 13:02:12